With Christ, your greatest pain becomes your greatest strength.

If you let Him, He will turn your pain into love and joy that serves and blesses others in ways you never thought possible.

With Him, your pain becomes your superpower.

It changes into deep, joyful, Real Love.

And Real Love never fails.

Ever.

What I Want My

Children

to Know

Before I Die

BY EKSAYN AARON ANDERSON

Acknowledgements

I feel deeply grateful

- to my wife and companion, Katie for her patience, insight, and encouragement and help in editing.

- to my sons and daughters, for teaching me more about love than I ever thought possible and for continuing to teach me how to be a better man and father. This book is for you.

- to my father, EksAyn Alan Anderson, for his unfailing optimism even when facing stage four lung cancer and for listening, praying for, and counseling with me tirelessly. He is my hero.

- to my mother, Patricia Anderson, for her example of consistency and strength.

- to my brother, Leland Anderson, for his thoughtful insights about education, parenting, and fatherhood.

- to my sister, Shalissa Lindsay, for her insights and suggestions and her ability to foresee and prevent problems.

- to my youngest brother, Bryce Anderson, for his networking talents and constant brotherly love.

- to my brothers and sisters for many wonderful memories.

- to Susan Glenn for her unparalleled patience and skill in coaching, and for creating and leading groups that bless myself and others.

- to Kim Dicou for her extremely thoughtful, detailed and insightful feedback.

- to Eric Aroca, Roscoe Allen, and Jesse Good for their consistently honest and constructive feedback.
- to Jimmy Nelson, for his lifelong friendship, example and feedback.
- to Jason Webb, for his legal advice, good humor and help in getting this book ready for print.
- to Brady Bastian for his encouragement, friendship and example of fatherhood.
- to Ron and Bonnie McMillan for valuable advice and insights and for their shining example of faith.
- to Solomon and Ayiba, for their examples of following Jesus.
- to Brent and Ilene Barton, for raising a wonderful daughter who is now my wife.
- to my late Grandma and Grandpa Stratford for raising my wonderful mother and for wonderful, wonderful memories.
- to my late Grandma and Grandpa Wille – for good memories, and many funny laughs.
- to my late Grandpa Anderson, who's "hoot owl's nest" in his camping trailer and his "Come in this house!" enthusiastic greetings will always be treasured memories.
- to my late Grandma Anderson and other countless ancestors who I never met, but whose influence is surely with me in ways I don't realize or comprehend.
- to Kevin for teaching me that when the student is ready the teacher will appear but when the student is truly ready the teacher will disappear.
- to Bruce Marshall for good advice and consistently seeing the positive in me.
- to Jeremy Pixton for his lifelong friendship.
- to Lara Kennedy for conscientious editing and advice.
- to Cindy C. Bennett for her artistic talents and formatting expertise.

I am grateful for the happy memory of my mother, Linda Lee Stratford Anderson, who, despite her death over three decades ago, continues to influence me with the little things she did, for wanting me to draw trees the way I see them, and for seeing the noble and good in me. Her soft and gentle influence continues to this day and blesses both me and my children all the time.

And finally, to Jesus Christ, who breathes life into everything and everyone.

My Dearest Children,

I have been working on writing a book for years and couldn't seem to figure out the exact direction that I wanted to take with it—until recently.

One morning I awoke and felt strongly that I needed to write a book to you—so that is what I am doing now.

I love you more than you know.

Whether I am in the flesh to tell you of my love or will one day have to show you in some other way from across the divide between life and death (this book is an attempt at just that), I pray you will know that your dad loved you, and still does.

And I always, always will.

Most would think that a parent's job is to teach their children, but many parents realize at some point that their children have really taught them the important things.

You have taught me more than you know. You have taught me how to truly love.

Nothing you do will ever keep me from loving you.

For my older children, the things I write in this book you have probably heard many, many times. For my younger children, you may not have been able to comprehend some of these things before now.

I realize my example often falls short of the principles I try to teach you. I have made many mistakes that I should not have made. I hope that you will learn from my mistakes so that you won't have to repeat them.

I don't know how long I will live, but I felt I should get this in print, so it cannot be lost or changed.

Life is all about relationships, and relationships are all about principles. And real principles can be learned and flow from the ultimate source, Jesus Christ.

The main thing to get in life is that Jesus is the Christ, and then strive with all your might to follow Him. He is the way out of any darkness you feel. He is the way out of this shadow of life and into the Real Place. He is the Way, the Life, and the Son of God. His words are both easy and hard. They are both an easy yoke and a cross to bear when following Him.

In your lifetime, there will likely be a maximum effort to discount, confuse, and counterfeit Jesus Christ. Keep believing in Jesus. Lose faith in any man or woman, but don't stop believing in Jesus. Or, if you have lost faith in Him for any reason—please, please continue and try with all your might to have faith in Him—even if it doesn't make sense.

He is Real.

My children, the most important work you do will be in your own homes. Be brave enough to get married and start a family, with children, if you can (if you can't, do your best to be parents to others who are lost or may have no functional parents). Be brave parents, submit yourselves to conscience, and teach your children to submit to conscience as well.

When I was younger, I wanted to change the world. I wanted to speak and write books that would move the masses. Somehow, over the years, I learned something that changed my desires—something profound. I read a phrase that seems to repeat itself in my mind. It says something like this:

"If you want to change the world, go home and love your family."[1]

Changing the world doesn't have to be in some big, grandiose way that is seen by others. In the words of Neal A. Maxwell:

> When the real history of mankind is fully disclosed, will it feature the echoes of gunfire or the shaping sound of lullabies? The great armistices made by military men or the peacemaking of women in homes and in neighborhoods? Will what happened in cradles and kitchens prove to be more controlling than what happened in congresses?[2]

---

[1] Often attributed to Mother Teresa. Some dispute whether the quote was actually said by her.

[2] Maxwell, Neal A., 2013, "The Women of God."

This book is for you, my children. I am feeling tingles as I write this:

Somehow, I know that you, my dear children, through your choices to be like Jesus, will change and be a light to the world.

Remember, when it is darkest, that is when the light is needed the most.

Your Dad

A note about my father:

Though this is a book written to my children, in some ways, it is also a book that I pray will honor both God and my parents. Ideally, a man learns how to be a man from his own father.

And for me, it would be disingenuous of me to not thank my dear father, EksAyn Alan Anderson.

He is a man of courage, honor, and of permanency.

When my mother passed away decades ago, leaving my father as a widower with seven young children, he could easily have chosen to become discouraged and stop following Jesus. Instead, it seemed to only strengthen his already strong resolve. This one choice alone, to be faithful when things were very hard, is having an effect so far and wide, it is impossible to quantify.

He teaches me each day with his example how to be a better man, husband and father. His noble choices to follow Jesus Christ deeply influence me, my brothers and sisters, and (currently) at least 53 grandchildren.

And his future influence I believe will be massive – we haven't even begun to see how his life choices will profoundly, if quietly, filter through coming generations. Centuries from now, people around the world who he will never meet, will be quietly blessed by the choices he has made in the past and makes presently.

My father is currently in a courageous battle against cancer, but you couldn't tell it from talking to him. His positivity, laughter, patience, and goodness shine through in a way that focuses the light of our Savior on others.

In so many ways, my fatherhood, my children, and the world, are affected by the great if unknown choices of my father.

Thank you, Dad.

There are many things that I would like my children to know that are not included in this book. This book includes things that I have chosen to share with both my children and the public.

This book is not necessarily designed to be read from front to back. It is more designed to let you skip around a bit. Like parenting, it is not always organized like you think it might be. There are thoughts that are short and to the point and there are thoughts that take more time to develop.

Life is messy—and so is this book.

Contents

Trees Grow Stronger in Storms 1

The Key to Heaven 37

The Wrong Side of the Door 51

The World Is Upside Down 53

This World Is *Not* It 69

Pattern of the King 79

Principles 81

More about Principles 87

Free Will and Real Love 91

Love Is the Answer 97

We Lead Our Feelings with Our Actions 99

The Most Important Thing to Remember When Teaching Others .. 105

The Importance of Family 109

Gods in Embryo versus Things 111

When I Discuss God with Friends 113

Turn the Other Cheek 117

Real Truth Exists 123

Fasting 125

The Little Things Are the Big Things 127

Starting the Day Out Right 139

Truth Mixed with Lies 141

Fear and Greed 147

Find Your Voice, Then Inspire Others to Do the Same 153

Just Do It 155

The Sacred Now 157

Satan's Counterfeits 159

Humility 161

The Best Way to Teach 165

Sustainable Growth 171

Time 173

If— 175

The Golden Rule 179

Acknowledgment and Recognition...................................... 185

The Center.. 187

Memorize Scriptures 189

Hidden Treasures 191

The Short-Term Hard Way Is the Long-Term Easy Way.................. 193

When the World Is Upside Down 201

Follow Your Promptings.. 203

Focus Brings Freedom... 207

Courage 211

Thoughts are Choices 213

Be Chaste and Virtuous.. 219

Honor Your Spouse 221

Start with Yourself First. 223

Trust God 227

Heaven Can Go Back in Time... 229

Do Good in Secret 231

You Are the CEO of Your Children's Education 233

Effort... 237

The Stage of Your Mind... 239

Confessing and Admitting Our Own Sins.......................... 241

Honor Your Father and Mother 243

Making Friends 245

Be Still 247

The Prerogative of the Brave... 249

Christ.. 251

Books and Other Media That I Recommend..................... 253

Works Cited... 255

Trees Grow Stronger in Storms

I don't have any formal credentials to write this book.

I don't have a PhD in any subject.

I am not a professional counselor.

I don't have decades of experience counseling families or helping marriages.

But there is at least one thing that happened long ago that set me on a journey that now compels me to take the time to share with you:

As an eight-year-old boy, I watched my mom die.

I know what life was like both before and after she died.

I know what she did decades ago that influences me today.

I know what she did decades ago that is influencing the grandchildren she never met—you--my children. I see her influence in her seven children, even my youngest brother, who was only seven weeks old when she died. I see her influence in the children of my brothers and sisters, and I am convinced that her influence will go on for generations to come.

You see, from watching her die, and from seeing how life was before and after, I have learned for myself that what you do in your family will last longer and have far more influence in the long run than *anything else* you ever do in the world.

Let me show you just one reason why I believe this.

I had a wonderful mom.

She was intelligent, calm, and a great listener. She had big, dark brown eyes that seemed to sparkle with love and tenderness even when she wasn't saying anything. When she spoke, her warm voice and body language left me feeling the love she radiated both to me and others.

She would often sit with me at the kitchen counter when I got home from school, smiling and listening intently. She had a knack for "listening" with her eyes, and when she would ask questions, I could feel the love emanating from her sparkling, deep brown eyes.

Among other things, she supported and encouraged my love of drawing—something I did tirelessly. When I was very young, I used to love to draw trees. Not just "sort of" draw trees—I used to draw every branch, every leaf, every detail, with dozens of leaves. I drew them the way I saw them. It would take a long time to draw them, and they were detailed and beautiful. They might have looked something like this:

Later on, when I went to school, I saw how the other children drew trees: a simple trunk drawn with two lines and a puffy cloud to represent the leaves—something that could be drawn in a few seconds. They might have looked something like this:

Somehow, after seeing the way other children drew their trees, I decided that the detailed trees I drew weren't good enough. Something in me wanted to fit in and be like the other children, so I stopped drawing the detailed trees that I used to draw and started to draw trees like the other children.

I found out later that when my mother saw this, she cried.

Why would she cry? You can probably guess: I was giving up a part of my individuality, part of who I was, to be like other children. And her love for me, her true love for me to be me, caused her to cry.

Fast forward a few years to when I was almost nine years old. After attending one of my baseball games, my mother complained of a severe headache. Concerned, my father took her to the hospital.

Before they left, I remember telling my mother, "I love you," and holding her tight in my eight-year-old arms.

I asked a relative who happened to be visiting us that day if my mom was going to die. He reassured me that she was not going to die.

I wanted to believe him.

I stayed up late in hopes that my parents would return soon and let me know that all was well. Hour after hour passed, and they had not returned. I eventually fell asleep.

The next morning, I arose and left my bedroom, anxious to see my parents. As I walked into the family room next to my bedroom, I could see my father, who was surrounded by many friends and neighbors.

I walked to the other side of the room wanting to see my mother, but she was not there. I saw my father, tears streaming down his face. His voice choked, and through his tears, he explained that my mother was "going to leave us."

My mother had suffered a cerebral hemorrhage, was unconscious, and was being kept alive by a life support machine. I remember praying, pleading with God that He would spare my mother's life.

Later, we went and visited her at the hospital. My mother was what doctors sometimes refer to as "brain dead." She could only breathe with the help of tubes coming out of her nose connected to a machine that made her chest inflate and deflate in what seemed to me a very unnatural way; I could not hear her warm voice nor see the sparkle in her deep brown eyes.

A short time later, I watched as they unplugged my mother from life support. As the life left her body, she turned bluish.

It was terrifying.

She looked so unlike my loving mom.

Before we left the hospital, I remember wanting to give my mom a kiss, but I was afraid, as she didn't look like my mom.

I went and faked a kiss by kissing the air about an inch from her head and then left the room.

As an eight-year-old boy, I watched my mom die.

Here is my question for you:

How do you think I draw trees now?

Now I draw them the way I see them—

I draw them the way my loving mother would want me to draw them.

In fact, right now, *even as I am writing this book*, I am figuratively drawing trees the way I see them.

I am not writing this book to please you.

I am not writing this book to fulfill a need in the marketplace.

Much of what I say may offend you, rub you the wrong way, or irritate you.

I am writing this book, because I am going to "draw trees the way I see them."

And if you want to go really deep—my mom loved me enough to teach me to draw trees the way I see them.

Even though I haven't given my mom a hug in over three decades, there is something that is almost as good as giving your mom a hug.

It is feeling her influence.

And I can feel it as I write this right now—*even though she died over three decades ago.*

Why did my mom die?

I have asked this question many times. And I am reminded of something my grandmother (my mother's mother) said that has become a family motto:

"No matter what the question, love is the answer."

Wait.

What?

Then why is there so much pain in the world?

Could there be a loving God in heaven who somehow still allows so much pain?

Wouldn't a God who allows pain really not be a loving God?

Why would a loving God in heaven allow me to watch my mom die at the age of eight, when I was so tender, yet old enough to really know what was going on and thus feel the pain so exquisitely?

It is these questions, particularly questions about the amount of unexplained pain in the world, that cause many people to wonder if God is real and if He is even there.

Though I don't know all the reasons why I had to watch my mom die, the following from C.S. Lewis somehow rings true, deep within me:

Imagine yourself as a living house. God comes in to rebuild that house. At first, perhaps, you can understand what He is doing. He is getting the drains right and stopping the leaks in the roof and so on: you knew that those jobs needed doing and so you are not surprised. But presently he starts knocking the house about in a way that hurts abominably and does not seem to make any sense. What on earth is He up to? The explanation is that He is building quite a different house from the one you thought of—throwing out a new wing here, putting on an extra floor there, running up towers, making courtyards. You thought you were going to be made into a decent little cottage: but He is building a palace. He intends to come and live in it Himself.[3]

Is it possible that the pain you feel is actually helping you in ways you don't fully understand?

I am convinced that it is.

There *will* be many things that will be hard in life. Many things— expect it. Do not expect a life of easiness.

But why? What is the real reason?

Though we don't seek pain, pain from God is a gift. His pain is part of the process that transforms us from being a "decent little cottage" into a "palace."

The pain lets us feel compassion for others. Just like metal being purified and strengthened in a fiery furnace, pain refines us.

I am convinced that one day, we will bow before God and, with fuller hearts than we can imagine, thank Him for all the trials and pain that He let us experience, seeing how He made us into palaces that we could never have imagined on our own.

In fact, if you let Him work in you, I am convinced that the greatest pain you experience can become your greatest gift. God willing, it can become your superpower.

---

[3] Lewis, C.S., *Mere Christianity*, (US Harper Collins 1952), 205.

Remember that when things are hard, it is because God is putting us into situations where we "will have to be very much braver, or more patient, or more loving than [we] ever dreamed of being before" because "we have not yet had the slightest notion of the tremendous thing He means to make of us."[4]

Remember, that "the process will be long and in parts very painful," but He knows what he is doing.[5]

I know that life can be a struggle.

But there is something about the struggle.

The struggle makes you stronger.

When things get dark and hard—and they will—pray for help.

Pray that God will send angels.

And then have faith that He will and does—even if you don't know they are there.

Whether I am alive or not when you read this, believe that I pray to God to be an angel for you.

My daughter, and your sister, Cheyenne, was a beautiful, angel baby.[6]

She had soft, dark hair and beautiful, deep brown eyes—just like my mom.

She was a calm baby.

Really *calm*.

Oh sure, she could fidget and move around and seemed to always want to put the most available thing in her mouth, like most young babies. But there were a number of times when she was *very* calm.

---

[4] Lewis, *Mere Christianity*, 205
[5] Lewis, *Mere Christianity*, 206
[6] My daughter from a previous marriage.

It was almost uncanny how calm she was during these times.

I remember more than once she would just gaze up at me with a serene and deep calm. She would look so deeply into my eyes and stare into them calmly, almost like she was looking for something.

Sometimes I would just have to stop what I was doing so that I could look back into her deep brown eyes.

I was sitting in my car on the side of the road when I received a phone call.

I picked up the phone.

"Hello?" I asked.

"Is this EksAyn Anderson?" said a stranger's voice.

"Yes."

"Your daughter has drowned. You need to come to the hospital," the stranger said bluntly.

"What?" I said, my voice quivering.

"Your daughter has drowned. You need to come to the hospital," the stranger repeated.

I don't remember how the call ended.

Stunned, I somehow drove to the hospital.

Somehow, I found a place to park.

Somehow, I made my way into the hospital.

Somehow, I found the way to the correct room.

When I walked into the hospital room, I could see my nine-month-old baby daughter on a hospital bed.

She had tubes coming out of her nose.

It wasn't the first time I had seen someone I loved with tubes coming out of their nose.

I heard someone in the room say the words "brain dead."

That wasn't the first time I had heard those words either.

There were a lot of people in that room who were *not* calm.

I walked slowly up to the hospital bed and stood next to Cheyenne, putting my hand on the side of her upper arm, near her shoulder.

The moment I touched her tiny arm, something happened.

I felt *calm*.

Tears were streaming down my face. I'm sure my heart was racing, and at least some adrenaline was pumping through my veins.

But in my heart, there was a deep, deep calmness.

On some level, deep inside, I knew that Cheyenne was not going to make it.

I knew she was going to die.

From watching my mom die when I was eight years old, I knew the seriousness of the words "brain dead."

But somehow, in that moment, I felt very *calm*.

Deeply calm.

It was the same kind of calm that I would feel when she would look up at me as she would stare into my eyes, searching for something in me.

The emergency personnel in the room were moving slowly—not at all like you would probably envision a medical team rushing to save someone's life.

I approached one of the EMTs in the room. I needed more information.

"I'm a big boy. I need you to shoot straight and tell me what is going to happen with my daughter," I said directly, though politely.

"She is probably going to make a really good donor," he replied matter-of-factly, though with compassion.

I appreciated his straightforwardness. Though others would later call his comment insensitive, I never felt that way.

After a while, the medical personnel slowly wheeled my daughter out of the room and out toward a life-flight airplane, which was parked near the room we were in. They needed to fly Cheyenne a couple hundred miles or so to a specialized hospital.

I went on the life flight with her.

As the plane raced through the dark sky, I watched as they used a hand respirator to keep oxygen pumping through my daughter's unconscious body.

This wasn't the first time I had seen someone I love need help breathing.

I looked out the window and saw the darkened sky. I could feel the plane racing through the air thousands of feet above the ground.

I looked and saw my daughter and the emergency personnel huddled around her.

For just a brief moment, it seemed as if the darkness outside the plane was coming into me.

God, please don't let me become bitter, I prayed silently, tears streaming down my face.

That moment of prayer, that small moment in time, is etched into my mind forever.

I will never know the exact place where I offered up that prayer on that June day—somewhere racing through the air thousands of feet above the desert. I don't remember how long it took, though it seemed to be just an instant.

However, that moment was a critical moment for me—and my prayer was answered. I have not been bitter about my daughter's death, even once, since she died.

The plane landed.

My daughter and I were loaded onto an ambulance.

It drove with the emergency lights on, though without a siren. It drove slowly from the airport to the hospital.

There was no reason to hurry.

My daughter was brought in to the very large, new hospital. She was hooked up to all kinds of medical equipment. There were a handful of staff and doctors that went in and out.

The doctors and nurses were professional and kind.

Eventually, one of the doctors explained that the prognosis didn't look good, and the subject of donating her organs was brought up.

It was decided that Cheyenne would be an organ donor.

Hours later, it would be the second time in my life that I would watch someone I love be taken off a life-support system.

When they took her off the machine, I held my daughter in my arms.

Though nearly brain dead, she had just a bit of brain stem functioning, which allowed her to breathe just a bit, but in a very slow, strained way.

I held her as her belabored breathing slowly diminished.

I cradled her in my arms.

After a long while, her breathing stopped.

I just held her in my arms and cried.

My father is an example of permanency and consistency in my life. Despite losing his wife at a young age, and even as a widower with seven children, he was consistent and permanent in his determination to do what he felt was right. He did not become bitter after my mom died, nor did he become overwhelmed. He stayed steadfast and went forward with faith. He remarried a choice woman. Together with his new wife, he continued to teach us about Jesus and read scriptures with us. They took us on dozens of road trips that, taken together, spanned the entire country—from California to New York. We saw national and state parks, camped in dozens of beautiful campgrounds across the country, learned about and visited countless national historic and church sites. My dad spent time with us one on one and counseled us. He worked hard and taught us to work hard. He showed us by his example how to be devoted to family and to the gospel of Jesus Christ.

My father is about the best example of steadfastness you can find. It is hard not to get a sense of his permanency and his consistency when around him. He is an anchor to many who know him, especially to his own children and grandchildren.

For my entire childhood, my father read scriptures with us and taught us about Jesus Christ. He took me and my brothers and sisters to church each and every week. Nearly all our worship services happened in a church about a half mile from our home. That church, compared with the surrounding neighborhood and shopping center near it, was much older—it was roughly as old as my father. And like my father, it had a feeling of permanency, like it would always be there.

It was the church where my brothers and sisters and I attended each week. We were baptized at that church. We worshiped countless times at that church. We had weekly activities at that church. The church had a basketball court and a baseball diamond and a large field, which we used many times to recreate over the years. We had many family gatherings and reunions at that church.

I believe the church was originally built back when much of the area was a farming community, on a somewhat quiet road. Gradually, the area grew and grew. The streets were widened. Traffic increased exponentially. A steady stream of cars, trucks, and all kinds of vehicles now flow busily day and night in front of the church. New buildings, traffic lights, and a busy freeway surround it—what once was mainly farmland is now city.

I can't help but think that, in some ways, my dad is like the old church. Things around the church have changed a lot, but like my dad, the church hasn't.

The church and the land it was on stayed the same.

The church, like my dad, was a symbol of permanency. The church, like my dad, had consistently been a source of worship, fun activities, and deep heritage, despite anything that changed around it.

Like my dad, its foundation was built before I was born.

Like my dad, it served many, many people for decades.

Like my dad, it hosted many wonderful activities.

Like my dad, the church was a symbol of consistency and permanency.

Recently, it was announced that the old church would be torn down to make room for a breathtaking new temple.

I was saddened at the prospect of losing the church building I had made so many memories in. However, my father, upon learning the news, did not seem sad at all.

In fact, he was filled with excitement and joy. He was overjoyed. He was ecstatic.

To him, it mattered much less that the church was being torn down, because something so much better, a temple, was coming.

Close to this same time, my father had been experiencing some trouble in his lungs. Over the course of a few months, I had noticed my father's health seemed to be worsening. Eventually, my dad decided to go to the hospital to get checked out. He found that he needed to get his lungs drained of a fluid that had been building up in them, as it had become more difficult for him to breathe.

I decided to spend the night with my dad at the hospital while the doctors did tests to find out what was wrong.

I drove alone, and on this night I took a different road, one that I normally didn't take. It was a road that had a view of almost the entire valley, including twinkling city lights stretching for miles. In the distance, I could see the large hospital complex where my dad was staying. As I drove, something interesting happened. I could feel a warm, comforting sensation. It was very, very strong. I believe that feeling was the Holy Ghost. I could feel that something important was going to happen.

I stayed in the room with my dad that night, and it was a precious experience.

A day or so later, the results came back that my dad had stage-four lung cancer. I was there, at the hospital, when he found out.

I hugged my dad and cried. I didn't want to lose my dad.

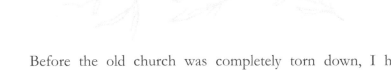

Before the old church was completely torn down, I had the opportunity to walk through it with my dad, who I now knew had cancer.

I cried as I walked through the old church, remembering memories of my mom and dad there. Somehow, the memories of my mom attending that church made its loss even more acutely painful. The thought of my dad's cancer was much harder for me than the thought of the church being torn down, but having them happen together hurt—and hurt deeply.

I stood in the church and cried. I hugged my dad.

In that moment, I could tell how important each moment really is. We pass through moments that, at least in this life, we will never be able to pass through again. I would never again be able to walk through that church—it has now been demolished. I wasn't sure how long I would be able to hug my dear father.

I could feel how important it was to cherish the time with my dad, with my wife, with my children, as time seems to move so quickly forward. The moments we share together are more valuable than anything else in the world.

Later, a thought came to me.

My dad's body was being torn down by cancer, and similarly, the church building we had made so many memories in was soon to be demolished.

That said, something else was at play: because Jesus Christ died for my dad, my dad's body will be changed from something like an old church to something more like the breathtaking new temple taking its place.

I couldn't help but cry when I first thought this.

Jesus and His love are the true rock. He is more permanent than my father's aging body, more permanent than my childhood home or church. When all we know has passed away, Christ will still be there. He is our true home.[7]

And because of Christ and my father's example of excitement, joy, and optimism, I, too, can choose to look forward with excitement and optimism.

My wife is a spiritual supermodel. Somehow, through God's grace, I ended up with her and she with me.

As of the time I am writing this, my wife has had five miscarriages. Four of them were to the point where she had to deliver our deceased children at the hospital.

Let me tell you about just one of these experiences:

A couple of years ago, my wife found out that she was pregnant with a baby girl.

---

[7] This thought first came to be when I heard Ali Lund in our local congregation share it.

She was both excited and scared.

Excited because she wanted to have a baby girl. Her excitement was compounded when she learned that three of her sisters-in-law were also due to have baby girls around the same time. She was so excited to think of them growing up as friends and cousins.

On the other hand, she was scared, because just several months before, she had needed to deliver our baby son who died prematurely in her womb, and she was afraid of it happening again.

It was around the same time my wife learned that she was going to have a baby girl, that I learned my dear father had lung cancer. It had progressed to the point where one of his lungs was in such trauma that the doctor could not hear any airflow in that lung.

Our emotions were a mix of bitter and sweet.

We felt excited that life was coming into the world (with our new baby girl on the way) and deeply saddened that my sweet father was suffering from cancer—and we dreaded the thought of his passing away.

A couple of months later, my father reported something interesting. He had been at a doctor's appointment with his oncologist (cancer doctor). While there, the doctor checked both lungs with a stethoscope, and the doctor was embarrassed to ask which lung had the cancer. In other words, the lung that had had no airflow before now seemed to be flowing about as well as the other lung—to the point where the doctor couldn't tell the difference without checking his records, which he apparently hadn't prior to the appointment with my father.

Miraculously, it seemed that my father's condition was better than before.

On the other hand, it wasn't too much later that my wife called me from the doctor's office, sobbing. She had just learned for the second time in one year that our unborn baby did not have a heartbeat. She was far enough along that the doctors would, again, have to deliver the baby girl, now dead, that my wife had so hoped for.

How fast things can change.

One thing I know:

Every person reading this book, and every person you will ever meet, has a battle, has pain, that you don't know about.

Everyone. You. Meet. Has. Pain. You. Cannot. See.

So here is a question: Why is life filled with so much pain?

My grandmother was right.

No matter the question, love really is the answer.

God lets us have pain precisely so that, if we let it, we can love more powerfully. Somehow our greatest pains become blessings that allow us to help and bless others.

This book is an attempt to use my own pain to love you, my children, as well as any others that might be reading this. I am crying as I write this. And I know that some of you may be crying too.

That's okay.

My mom, despite giving birth to and at least beginning to raise seven children before she died at age thirty-two, still found time to write in her journal. I treasure those journals. However, I do wish that I had even more access to her wisdom, her thinking, her thoughts, her advice.

And that is where this book comes in.

"We must be the change we wish to see in the world."[8]

Writing this book is a small attempt at trying to "be the change" myself, as I am trying to pass on as much of my thinking, my thoughts, as I can to my children and others.

If you are experiencing pain, please know that it is not an accident—we are *not* just some accident of the cosmos. Nor is it because God is bad.

It is because you are loved.

And, God willing, you will be able to use it to love others in ways you may not yet comprehend.

Life breaks us. But if we, as broken people, will accept and follow His Son, God redeems the broken. He then makes us much, much stronger at the broken places.

He allows us to be broken so that we can "be the change we wish to see in the world."

---

[8] Often attributed to Mahatma Gandhi. Some dispute whether the quote was actually said by him.

We *get* to *be* the change.

And I believe that God is making us into the change He and the world need—for reasons we don't yet understand fully.

My children, and any others who may read this book, when the pain comes, and it will, pray to let God tell you how to use it to love others. He uses pain in ways we cannot often understand in the moment. But trust Him. He will heal you. And when He does, you will be able to serve others much more than you may have dreamed.

He is making you into something you may never have even dreamed possible.

I know in life that I have had more than one guardian angel—you've just read about some of them. My mom. My Cheyenne. Our babies that haven't made it. Countless others that I can feel God has sent. Many of the angels we have are alive now—my wife and my father are angels to me. You, my children, are angels to me.

Whether I am living or dead when you read this, know that I will do everything I can to be "there" for you, even if I cannot be physically there for you in life.

And *please* remember the words of my mother's mother:

No matter the question, *Love Is the Answer.*

The Key to Heaven

The principles of mercy and justice are key.[9]

I believe that heaven is filled with people who both forgive and have been forgiven. Heaven comes as we learn to show mercy for others even when we could demand fairness and justice.

The story of Jean Valjean in *Les Miserables*[10] is considered a classic. This story is timeless because the principles interwoven in it speak to our deep selves—the same deep part of ourselves that unconsciously knows truth from another life, another time—when we lived with God. These truths seem to wash up again and again on the shores of our consciousness precisely because some truths are so potent that it matters not how thick the veil is that guards our former life with God.

The story begins with Jean Valjean stealing bread to feed a starving nephew. He is caught and sentenced to jail and hard labor and ended up being there for nineteen years. When finally released, he finds that the world is hostile toward him, an unwanted convict, and so he goes door-to-door in search of a place to stay. At one point, he knocks on the door of a kind priest. The priest invites him in and feeds him and gives him a bed to sleep in. Though Jean Valjean is likely thankful for a place to stay and eat, he still feels like a convict and, used to being thought of as a

---

[9] Proverbs 3:3–4.

[10] Hugo, Victor, *Les Miserables*, (Lacroix, Verboeckhoven & Cie, 1862).

thief, lives up to the expectation. He decides to steal from the priest—concealing the priest's silverware and sneaking out of his home.

Shortly thereafter, Jean Valjean gets arrested, and the police find the stolen silverware with the priest's markings on the silver. Thinking that they have caught a thief, the police bring Jean Valjean, and the silver, back to the kindly priest, wanting confirmation of their suspicions.

When the priest comes to the door and finds the police with the accused Jean Valjean, the police ask if the silver is, indeed, his.

What happens next is extraordinary.

Instead of the anger and indignation typical of one who has been robbed, the priest *decides in that moment that he has already given Jean Valjean the silver.* Then, in true Christlike fashion, the priest goes back into the house and retrieves even more silver, giving it to the thief as well.

The police, and the thief himself, watch, astounded.

The police, now with no case to pursue, leave, with Jean Valjean now a free man.

As the priest and Jean Valjean now find themselves alone, the priest quietly tells Jean Valjean that this is his chance to make himself an honest man.

Jean Valjean has never before experienced such mercy. It goes against everything that he has learned in society—it goes against all he has learned in prison doing hard labor.

This one act of kindness changes everything for Jean Valjean—it changes his very soul.

He is no longer a criminal, but becomes a great man. He becomes a leader in the community, a businessman, and very compassionate. He saves a child whose mother has died and spends the rest of his life protecting her and giving her a great life, all the while a model citizen. He lives up to the potential that the priest saw in him.

The one Christlike act of the priest spreads not only to Jean Valjean but to others.

This story is really the key to heaven. It's a story that repeats itself in all the best literature and scripture.

It is the story of true love.

It is really our story.

It's the story of God loving us. The details may be different, but we are all in the same predicament.

We are all sinners and have sinned. The principle of fairness would imply that we deserve to be imprisoned and jailed. Christ frees us. He runs and gets the silver even though we do not deserve it. He died for our sins even though we did not deserve it. And like Jean Valjean, we now have a chance to make ourselves honest and better men and women.

He is getting the silver for us every single day, and He wants us to learn to do the same for others.

Every day, if we really look for it, we are given many chances to run back in and get more silver and give it away OR to demand fairness and justice be done. Every day we choose between heaven and hell. When we condemn the thoughtless things our spouse/coworkers/children/or even politicians do, it is like we are saying, "Police, this man/woman is a robber and deserves to go to jail." When we, despite the fact that their thoughtlessness or malice has "stolen our silverware," run back in and give them more, we open the door to heaven.

Let's break this down.

At the root of this story are two seemingly contradictory ideas— justice and mercy. The sense of wanting things to be fair comes because we are literally the children of the most just and fair Being in the universe—God Himself. Because we are His children, this idea of fairness is found in every religion, culture, and on every continent. It comes intrinsically.

Interestingly, the idea of mercy is also found almost everywhere— most people want mercy, especially for themselves. Like fairness, this sense of wanting mercy comes because we are literally the children of the most merciful Being in the universe—God Himself.

Our God is both as merciful as it gets and as just as it gets—He spans the whole.

The problem is that many, if not most, in the world have the attitude of "mercy for me, justice for you." If we are honest with ourselves, we often hold people to a different standard than we hold ourselves. This attitude is found nowhere at all in the Real World.

God inverts this attitude . His attitude is "justice for me, mercy for you," and Jesus Christ actually embodies this. Jesus took upon Himself the whole weight of justice when He died for our sins. He then extends unbelievable mercy to us by patiently asking us and allowing us time to, like Jean Valjean, become honest men.

God wants us to become like Him. And that means we get to change. Forefront among the personal attitudes we need to change is this:

"Mercy for me, justice for you"

to

"Justice for me, mercy for you"

Let's examine further:

Jean Valjean stole the priest's silver. It would have been fair to have Jean Valjean return the silver and then pay a price to the community for violating the laws of that community.

The priest was given full opportunity to demand this fairness. He could have demanded the silver back (justice) and then asked that the thief be taken to jail. In today's words, he could have "pressed charges."

But he didn't.

This is where it gets interesting.

Instead, the priest showed mercy. He went inside and got more silver and gave it to Jean Valjean, saying Valjean had forgotten it. His act threw out and went above the idea of fairness and showed mercy—in front of Valjean's accusers, the police.

And this is exactly what God and Christ have done for us. We know we have done things that deserve punishment. God and Jesus know too. But they have decided to give us the chance to make ourselves "honest men" like Jean Valjean. Jesus Christ did the ultimate act of running in to get the silver by dying for our sins—by paying a debt for us.

I pray we can realize what a big, big deal this is. It is literally the biggest and best thing that ever happened in the entire universe.

This life is the chance to practice being like Jesus. It is going to constantly serve up situations that seem unfair. If we stay close to the Holy Ghost, we will feel when we need to go back in and get the silver for others.

If we are going to get to heaven, I believe we have got to give up the idea of fairness for ourselves—at least for now. God is perfectly just and will repay as He sees fit. We have to find and consciously seek out opportunities to figuratively run back into the house and get more silver. These opportunities lie everywhere, in our interactions with our spouses, children, and others we come in contact with.

We like things to be fair here and now, but they are not. If life were truly fair, we would not like it. We would all be in hell. And the only way out of hell, in our relationships and in life, is to extend the mercy to others that we so desperately need ourselves. We need to extend goodness to people who we may feel are unworthy of goodness.

Jean Valjean did not deserve the extra silver—he had just stolen from the priest.

Likewise, a belittling spouse, an angry teenager, or a dishonest employee may not deserve our mercy. But the key to heaven lies in giving opportunities (led by the Holy Ghost) to appropriately "give them the silver" anyway. It's a higher law and acknowledges that God will ultimately give justice, not us. The law works *not* because it makes sense on the surface—because, on the surface, it doesn't.

But the God of all—the God who knows all about what lies beneath the surface of a soul, who has made and knows our very deepest selves, has asked us to run back in and get the silver for others. He has asked us to put our idea of fairness for ourselves (at least for now) aside.

Strive to be fair with others. Be kind. Keep your agreements. Be honest, upfront, and fair in your dealings with others.

That said, as a general rule, demand more "fairness" and "mercy" for others than you demand for yourself. This is not to say that you should be weak and allow people to walk all over you. I am not saying that at all. What I am saying is that to consciously and willingly let things be unfair for ourselves requires incredible strength—strength that very few of us have but which Christ embodied, and which with His help we can develop. The strongest Being ever to exist let things be unfair for Him. He saw our souls and loved them enough to let things be unfair for Him and in doing so somehow unlocked the key for us all to go to heaven—if we choose to follow Him.

What I am saying is that you can try to value people's souls more than you value things being "fair" for you. If you try with all your might to see people as God sees them, you will find that the Holy Ghost will, at times, prompt you to let things be unfair for you. Like the kindly priest, you will feel, at times, to get the silver for others—to do something that lets them know that their soul is of way more value than a shiny metal.

The Holy Ghost may also prompt you at times to do otherwise. Listen to and stay close to the Holy Ghost so that you know when to get the silver. There may be times when the Holy Ghost tells you not to get the silver. It is so important to stay close to the Holy Ghost.

Trying to see people like God sees them may help you rid the idea that you deserve a fair life. God is perfectly just. But it is up to us to let Him take care of the justice, not us.

Jesus made this clear when he said:

> Therefore is the kingdom of heaven likened unto a certain king, which would take account of his servants.
>
> And when he had begun to reckon, one was brought unto him, which owed him ten thousand talents. But forasmuch as he had not to pay, his lord commanded him to be sold, and his wife, and children, and all that he had, and payment to be made. The servant therefore fell down, and worshipped him, saying, Lord, have patience with me, and I will pay thee all. Then the lord of that servant was moved with compassion, and loosed him, and forgave him the debt.

But the same servant went out, and found one of his fellowservants, which owed him an hundred pence: and he laid hands on him, and took him by the throat, saying, Pay me that thou owest. And his fellowservant fell down at his feet, and besought him, saying, Have patience with me, and I will pay thee all. And he would not: but went and cast him into prison, till he should pay the debt. So when his fellowservants saw what was done, they were very sorry, and came and told unto their lord all that was done.

Then his lord, after that he had called him, said unto him, O thou wicked servant, I forgave thee all that debt, because thou desirest me: Shouldest not thou also have had compassion on thy fellowservant, even as I had pity on thee? And his lord was wroth, and delivered him to the tormentors, till he should pay all that was due unto him.

So likewise shall my heavenly Father do also unto you, if ye from your hearts forgive not every one his brother their trespasses.[11]

In the scriptures above, it was not fair to the king for him to forgive his servant the massive debt of ten thousand talents. Nor was it fair that the servant should give up the tiny one hundred pence that he was owed. But the whole story is basically saying that we should run back in the house and find more silver.

Life is not fair.

Ironically, life will actually be easier once this fact is accepted.

Life is intentionally designed to serve up all kinds of unfair circumstances, so that we can learn to truly love others. Learning to truly love others like Christ did is the ultimate *everything*. And so, if we get the ultimate *everything*—true Christlike love—we will eventually see that this school of life is

---

[11] Matthew 18:23–35.

infinitely more than fair—and in our favor—than we can possibly comprehend, though it almost certainly won't seem like it in the moments of injustice and pain.

As we learn to love, even in moments of immense injustice, we become more like Christ. He knows all about immense injustice and love.

Christ set the example. He is the way to the Real World. While delivering the Sermon on the Mount, Christ gave us the key to heaven:

> Ye have heard that it hath been said, An eye for an eye, and a tooth for a tooth:[12]

Christ basically acknowledges that the whole idea of fairness is one you've probably heard about. In the old days, if someone poked your eye out, fairness would say it is okay to poke out theirs. If they break your tooth off, fairness would say you should break off theirs.

> But I say unto you, That ye resist not evil: but whosoever shall smite thee on thy right cheek, turn to him the other also.[13]

Nothing about this is fair in any way. Doesn't it seem fair to resist when someone does something evil to us? But Christ is asking us *not* to fight back. In fact, he is telling us to let them harm us more—doesn't sound fair to me.

> And if any man will sue thee at the law, and take away thy coat, let him have thy cloak also.[14]

Nothing fair about this.

> And whosoever shall compel thee to go a mile, go with him twain.[15]

Nor this.

---

[12] Matthew 5:38.
[13] Matthew 5:39.
[14] Matthew 5:40.
[15] Matthew 5:41.

> Give to him that asketh thee, and from him that would
> borrow of thee turn not thou away.[16]

The command to give to others is not related to whether or not they deserve it. He did NOT add "as long as it is fair."

> Ye have heard that it hath been said, Thou shalt love thy
> neighbour, and hate thine enemy. But I say unto you,
> Love your enemies, bless them that curse you, do good
> to them that hate you, and pray for them which
> despitefully use you, and persecute you;[17]

Do you mean that if Jean Valjean "curses" me by stealing my silver, I should still bless him with more silver?

I believe the Christian answer is *yes*. It's not about the silver, it's about his soul—which is much, much more valuable.

> That ye may be the children of your Father which is in
> heaven: for he maketh his sun to rise on the evil and on
> the good, and sendeth rain on the just and on the
> unjust.[18]

He reminds us that allowing things to not be fair and still doing good toward our enemies is *how* we become God's children. He reminds us that God both makes the sun shine and sends rain on evil *and* good people, and to be His children, we need to follow His example.

What is fair about that?

Nothing. But guess what, you and me getting into heaven? Nothing fair about that either.

The next three verses are possibly three of the most important scriptures ever given:

> For if ye love them which love you, what reward have
> ye? do not even the publicans the same? And if ye salute

---

[16] Matthew 5:42.
[17] Matthew 5:43-44.
[18] Matthew 5:45.

your brethren only, what do ye more than others? do not even the publicans so?

Be ye therefore perfect, even as your Father which is in heaven is perfect. [19]

I love reading this last verse about being perfect—*in context* with all ten of the other verses that precede it. So many people read verse 48 alone and then get discouraged when they read it, as it tells them to be perfect. But if taken in context with verses 38 through 48, it is clear that verse 48 is just the final line of the "paragraph"—the nine verses before it. It beautifully shows how being perfect is really just a function of loving others even when it isn't fair—like you and me being loved by God and Christ, when we really did nothing of ourselves to deserve it.

Nothing about hanging on a cross and dying for people who hate you is fair. Keep that in mind the next time you feel like insisting that your spouse or children or coworkers treat you fairly.

Douglas Weiss, in his book *Servant Marriage*, says, "The attitude of fairness is so seductive at the beginning. I want you to know fairness is a cancer. If you start this, it can ultimately culminate in the destruction of your marriage, or at least make your marriage significantly less happy than if you were both servants who understood life and marriage were not fair (not even supposed to be fair). You must both sacrifice your lives for the marriage to be awesome."[20]

Why aren't things always fair?

To *truly* love others, you have to let go of the need to have things be fair.

Again, the God who knows all about what lies beneath the surface of each soul, who has made and knows our very deepest selves, has asked us to run back in and get more silver for others. He has asked us to put our idea of fairness for ourselves (at least for now) aside.

Why?

---

[19] Matthew 5:46–48.
[20] Weiss, Douglas, *Servant Marriage*, (Discovery Press, 2015).

My guess is that my grandmother was right: "No matter the question, love is the answer."

Notice that when the priest saw Jean Valjean, he helped him. He did NOT say:

"Why don't you go get a job?"

Or think to himself:

"The guy is a criminal, so he gets what he deserves."

Or:

"If I help him, he will never learn and just keep being a beggar."

This is important.

The priest just helped him, which, per Jesus Christ Himself, happens to be the criteria for how we will be judged, by the True Judge, at the last day:

> When the Son of man shall come in his glory, and all the holy angels with him, then shall he sit upon the throne of his glory: And before him shall be gathered all nations: and he shall separate them one from another, as a shepherd divideth his sheep from the goats: And he shall set the sheep on his right hand, but the goats on the left.
>
> Then shall the King say unto them on his right hand, Come, ye blessed of my Father, inherit the kingdom prepared for you from the foundation of the world: For I was an hungred, and ye gave me meat: I was thirsty, and ye gave me drink: I was a stranger, and ye took me in: Naked, and ye clothed me: I was sick, and ye visited me: I was in prison, and ye came unto me.
>
> Then shall the righteous answer him, saying, Lord, when saw we thee an hungred, and fed thee? or thirsty, and

gave thee drink? When saw we thee a stranger, and took thee in? or naked, and clothed thee? Or when saw we thee sick, or in prison, and came unto thee?

And the King shall answer and say unto them, Verily I say unto you, Inasmuch as ye have done it unto one of the least of these my brethren, ye have done it unto me.

Then shall he say also unto them on the left hand, Depart from me, ye cursed, into everlasting fire, prepared for the devil and his angels: For I was an hungred, and ye gave me no meat: I was thirsty, and ye gave me no drink: I was a stranger, and ye took me not in: naked, and ye clothed me not: sick, and in prison, and ye visited me not.

Then shall they also answer him, saying, Lord, when saw we thee an hungred, or athirst, or a stranger, or naked, or sick, or in prison, and did not minister unto thee?

Then shall he answer them, saying, Verily I say unto you, Inasmuch as ye did it not to one of the least of these, ye did it not to me. And these shall go away into everlasting punishment: but the righteous into life eternal.[21]

Help all the people you can.

And when you do help, give to the point that it hurts.

> I believe that Jesus hides all kinds of hidden treasures along the way for them that follow His words.

Remember, what we think is ours is not really ours; it is His. All the things we have are only things that are in our stewardship at the moment; we don't really "own" them (remember, the only thing that we really "own" is our ability to choose). I believe when we give, even when it hurts, the Lord opens the way for us to give even more. It doesn't make sense, but I believe it happens.

---

[21] Matthew 25:31-46.

When people choose to give, even when it is inconvenient or "hurts," somehow what they have increases. When they withhold from others, what they have often diminishes.

This phenomenon was written about thousands of years ago in the Bible:

> There is that scattereth, and yet increaseth; and there is that withholdeth more than is meet, but it tendeth to poverty.
> The liberal soul shall be made fat: and he that watereth shall be watered also himself.[22]

This phenomenon continues today, if the Lord wills it.

Don't give so that you will have more, because doing that isn't the reason for giving.

Just give. Stretch. Give more than is convenient.

And watch how God will make it okay for you, even if it doesn't seem like things will be okay in the moments before you give. Sometimes we have to give more than we think we can, not knowing how it will work out for ourselves.

C.S. Lewis, in *Mere Christianity*, wrote,

> I do not believe one can settle how much we ought to give. I am afraid the only safe rule is to give more than we can spare.[23]

Then, don't give up the opportunity to give because you are judging someone. Mother Teresa said, "If you judge people, you have no time to love them." She also said,

> I see Jesus in every human being.
>
> I say to myself, this is hungry Jesus, I must feed him. This is sick Jesus. This one has leprosy or gangrene; I must wash him and tend to him. I serve because I love Jesus.[24]

---

[22] Proverbs 11:24–25.

[23] Lewis, *Mere Christianity*, 86.

[24] Mother Teresa Quotes, GoodReads.

Think of every beggar, every person you see who needs help, as Jesus in disguise.

Because they are.

The Wrong Side of the Door

In his book, *The Weight of Glory*, C.S. Lewis wrote:

> *At present we are on the outside of the world, the wrong side of the door.* We discern the freshness and purity of morning, but they do not make us fresh and pure. We cannot mingle with the splendours we see. But all the leaves of the New Testament are rustling with the rumour that it will not always be so. *Some day, God willing, we shall get in.*[25]

There have been times in my life when I have felt someone from the other side of the door.

I have felt His presence.

I have felt His urge to call out to others.

This book is an attempt to do just that.

And I pray with all my heart that someday, if God wills it, we will find ourselves on the right side of the door.

---

[25] Lewis, *The Weight of Glory*, (ed. Walter Hooper, Macmillan Publishers, 1980), 43, emphasis added.

The World Is Upside Down

But he that is greatest among you shall be your servant.
And whosoever shall exalt himself shall be abased; and he that
shall humble himself shall be exalted.[26]

The world is upside down.

That's right.

Completely upside down (please note, there is a Real World, which, incidentally, is right side up).

Here is just one example (of many):

I have heard many people refer to a stay-at-home parent as "just" a stay-at-home parent, as if it were something unimportant, small, and menial. In fact, stay-at-home parents are often looked down on by parents employed outside the home.

They are seen by many as less contributing, less capable, less of almost everything. Some wonder why a parent would choose to stay home. If they were more capable, wouldn't they be out in the workforce, contributing their talents to the good of the world?

But that is the lie.

The truth is, to be a stay-at-home parent is to truly have the ultimate career.

---

[26] Matthew 23:11–12.

I don't say that lightly.

The.

Ultimate.

Career.

Why?

The small things a stay-at-home parent does or does not do each day will either benefit or harm not only her children, but their children— her children's children—and countless generations to come *in ways that no other job on the planet can.*

Yet this upside-down world seems to place more emphasis on worldly careers, titles, and positions--things that the Real World cares nothing for. As I write this, the title of CEO seems to command much more respect in this flipped world than that of stay-at-home parent.

However, let's break down the long-term influence of a CEO and compare it with the long-term influence of a stay-at-home parent.

The BBC reported that the average lifespan of a company in the prestigious S&P 500 is a short fifteen years, a sobering statistic for a CEO, or anyone, for that matter, working long hours in any business.

Incidentally, the overall trend seems to be that the average lifespan of a corporation is decreasing.[27]

It seems that only a very small fraction of companies in existence today will still exist thirty years from now, and if they do, it is quite likely that the business will do something completely different from what it is doing now.

Imagine for a moment a very successful CEO at a seemingly unstoppable company, who is making lots of money. Consider that the company likely will, within a short decade or two, be at least one of the following:

bought

sold

out of business

bankrupt

---

[27] Gittleson, Kim, (CNN 2012), "Can a Company Live Forever?"

disrupted

Now, compare that to the role of a stay-at-home father or mother:

This is likely harder to see, precisely because the interactions are hidden from the view of almost everyone.

Often, even the stay-at-home parent doesn't realize the effect he or she is having. Let me tell you a story from my own life to illustrate.

I remember a moment with my mother in the red-carpeted hallway of our home. There was nothing particularly special about being with my mom in that hallway—it was a regular family meeting place. It was used for lots of things: riding on my father's back like a horse with my siblings after he got home from work, playing blocks with my brother, and praying together as a family were just a few of many family moments that happened in that hallway.

But this particular moment was a moment when I was alone with my mother. Her words still ring in my ears: "Eks, I want you to know that I know the Church is true." It was a moment without fanfare or pomp. She didn't tell me this during a family home evening or a family scripture study. It was a quiet, calm moment just between us that took about five seconds or less.

It was only a few years later that my mother passed away suddenly from a cerebral hemorrhage.

Even though my mother passed away more than three decades ago, her influence is with me still. I have made my fair share of mistakes, as well as many good choices, since she passed away, *but I can still hear her words to me in that hallway.*

Sometimes, it seems, the business of life can crowd out what is important. We may think we have to do something big to make a lasting difference in our children's lives. But this is not the case.

We may think that we have to wait for some magical teaching moment.

But we don't.

Perhaps all we need is five seconds and a few words in a hallway.

I doubt my mom knew at the time how long that moment would last in my mind, or how it would influence her grandchildren decades later.

This moment was hidden from everyone but me and my mother. Hidden.

I am reminded what Jesus himself said about things that are *hidden*:

> Again, the kingdom of heaven is like unto treasure *hid* in a field; the which when a man hath found, he *hideth*, and for joy thereof goeth and selleth all that he hath and buyeth that field.[28]

And further:

> The kingdom of heaven is like unto leaven, which a woman took, and *hid* in three measures of meal, till the whole was leavened.[29]

Much of that which is from heaven is hidden in this overturned world.

This world parades the five seconds that happen when leadership from a company walks out on the balcony of the NASDAQ and rings the bell (the ringing of the bell signifies that the company is now trading publicly for the first day).

Our inverted world values these moments with press, pictures, and fanfare. The moment when my mom told me she knew the Church was true was experienced by just my mom and myself. Again, it was hidden.

Yet the hidden moment in the hallway with my mom influences the choices I make and who I am becoming, which in turn is influencing my children, and will continue to influence generations to come.

In contrast, the moment on the NASDAQ will be paraded in the media and valued by many for a while but will soon fade and be forgotten when the business is bought, sold, bankrupted, or disrupted, likely within a decade or two (and if current trends continue, perhaps sooner than that).

In other words, the *long-term* effect a CEO has, despite the visibility and glamour of the job, will pale in comparison to the *long-term* effect of

---

[28] Matthew 13:44, emphasis added.
[29] Matthew 13:33, emphasis added.

a stay-at-home parent. She is literally, minute by minute, building the next generation, and thus strongly influencing the generations that follow. Her choice of how to care for, listen to, read to, educate, and love her own children will be the pattern they will generally follow when shaping the next generation. Her choices will influence children hundreds and even thousands of years from now.

Please note that most CEOs make wonderful contributions. Their insights and decisions often create a plethora of jobs, opportunities, and many good things in the world. These jobs and opportunities can help feed many families, sometimes feeding families around the globe. Many, if not most, CEOs are devoted to their families and the communities in which they live. I know of many CEOs who are fabulous people, contribute generously to wonderful causes, and are huge forces for good in the world.

In addition, many parents, both single and married, work hard to provide for their families, often working long hours. Some of these parents may not be able to stay home with their children, for various reasons, even if they would like to. I honor these parents. Their goodness and sacrifice are real.

Many wonderful parents have to juggle the work they do at home and the work in their careers. Much of the work they do is good and noble. Sometimes they are forced to choose between work and family. The point is that the work you do *in* your own home will outlast any contribution you make *outside* your home. *Make your choices with this in mind.*

Neal A. Maxwell asked important questions:

> When the real history of mankind is fully disclosed, will it feature the echoes of gunfire or the shaping sound of lullabies? The great armistices made by military men or the peacemaking of women in homes and in neighborhoods? Will what happened in cradles and kitchens prove to be more controlling than what happened in congresses?[30]

And, again, from Neal A Maxwell:

---

[30] Maxwell, "The Women of God."

Some mothers in today's world feel "cumbered" by home duties and are thus attracted by other more "romantic" challenges. Such women could make the same error of perspective that Martha made. The woman, for instance, who deserts the cradle in order to help defend civilization against the barbarians may well later meet, among the barbarians, her own neglected child.[31]

As a wise man, David O. McKay, quoted:

The home is the first and most effective place for children to learn the lessons of life: truth, honor, virtue, self-control; the value of education, honest work, and the purpose and privilege of life. Nothing can take the place of home in rearing and teaching children, and no other success can compensate for failure in the home.[32]

Dallin H. Oaks, quoting J.F. Smith, said:

"After all, to do well those things which God ordained to be the common lot of all man-kind, is the truest greatness. To be a successful father or a successful mother is greater than to be a successful general or a successful statesman.

"Success in an occupation—even a lofty one—is only temporary," President Smith concluded, whereas success as a parent is "universal and eternal greatness."

Despite the importance of our task, these are difficult times for parents. The stresses and problems of modern living pose great problems for parents. These are

---

[31] Maxwell, Neal A., (Deseret Book, 1977), *Wherefore Ye Must Press Forward*, 102.
[32] James E. McCulloch, "Home: The Savior of Civilization" [1924], 42; in Ensign, May 1935, 116

suggested by the bittersweet definition of a family as "a group of people who have keys to the same house."

The popular terms "women's liberation" and "men's liberation" suggest other problems. This kind of "liberation" often purports to free men and women from family responsibilities. Men or women who desert or neglect their families may be liberated from responsibilities but they are imprisoned by sin. Whatever may happen in the short run, no one can ever achieve true liberation or freedom by fleeing eternal responsibilities. Eternal freedom requires the conscientious fulfillment of family responsibilities.[33]

You may not realize it, but your life is currently *massively* affected by the choices your parents' parents' parents made. The choices they made, the kinds of parents they were, currently affect you in ways that are impossible to measure. More importantly, the career they had outside the home is likely affecting you *significantly less* than the kind of parent they were.

It likely doesn't matter to you if your great-great-grandparents had the coolest job or house, horse or plow. But the kind of parent they were is affecting you right now—because it affected your parents' parents—which affected your parents. And, like it or not, it is affecting you.

What did your great-great-grandparents do for a living?

My guess is you don't know (even if you do know, remember, you have sixteen great-great-grandparents—do you know what all sixteen did?) If you are like many people I have asked this question, it is likely that you do not know and do not even really care.

Here is my next question. Do you know what *kind of a parent* your great-great-grandparents were?

Again, you may answer no. You may say that you don't even care.

But you may "know" more than you think you know.

---

[33] Oaks, Dallin H., 1985, "Parental Leadership in the Family."

Let me illustrate this with something I have observed in my family:

My nine-year old son tends to be great at saving money. I happen to know that he learned this from my wife--who tends to be very frugal and conservative financially. When I've talked to my wife about this, she recalls that she learned it from her mother, and then goes even further, recalling how her now-deceased grandma used to say: "Use it up, wear it out, make it do, or do without." Upon further research, her grandma learned it from her own mother.

From what I can tell, this tendency to be frugal has literally been passed down for *at least* 5 generations – though possibly for much more than that. It is affecting my son today.

My son couldn't articulate why he is good at saving money. He would probably just say it is a good idea. But the truth is that my son is being influenced by a woman both he and I never met. A woman born in the late 1800's is influencing my son now in the 2020's.

She died over half a century ago, but her influence didn't.

Let me share another more obvious example: Somewhere in my ancestry, hundreds of years ago, more than one of my ancestors chose to come from Europe to America. This choice not only affects where I was born and now live, but it has massively influenced the language I speak, the education, culture, and even religion that I now experience.

In much the same way, the type of parent your great-great-grandparent was, whether you like it or not, is *affecting you today.* You may not realize it, but it is *very* real nonetheless. And by the same token, *the way you raise your children will affect generations after you.*

Here is the good news and the bad news:

Your choices as a parent are more powerful than you can imagine.

What you are doing in your home right now may very well be passed down for generations. Whether you like it or not, your parenting choices in your home today may bless or curse people you will never meet in this life – your children's children's children's children.

Again, parenting, even though it is often looked down on in this world, is actually the *ultimate career*—a career that will have more long-lasting effects than any other—including that of any business leader, or any other job, for that matter.

Parenting is *it*.

Consider this quote from C.S. Lewis in his book *Miracles*:

> In the Christian story God descends to re-ascend . . . He goes down to come up again and bring the whole ruined world up with Him. One has the picture of a strong man stooping lower and lower to get himself underneath some great complicated burden. He must stoop in order to lift, he must almost disappear under the load before he incredibly straightens his back and marches off with the whole mass swaying on his shoulders . . .
>
> In this descent and re-ascent everyone will recognise a familiar pattern: a thing written all over the world . . . *go down to go up—it is a key principle. Through this bottleneck, this belittlement, the highroad nearly always lies.*[34]

Now, consider how something considered lowly in this world, like parenting, is exactly like the principle of going down to go up. A stay-at-home parent stays home to do a seemingly glamorless job—changing diapers, preparing food, perhaps cleaning and vacuuming.

But mixed in with all this are magical moments hidden from those who haven't experienced it.

Many stay-at-home parents know the priceless but unpublicized moment their child smiles for the first time, says her first word, or giggles for the first time.

These magic moments may come when she feels to teach her child something or when her child is ready to learn and asks searching questions.

They are woven in and out of the very fabric of the child's young life and are mixed in with the diapers, food preparation, cleaning, and vacuuming.

The way she responds to these hidden moments and opportunities for learning will affect not only her children but children hundreds and

---

[34] Lewis, C.S., *Miracles*, (1947), 111-112.

thousands of years from now. It's this pattern of being humble enough to simply be a good parent, this pattern of descending to reascend, that, as C.S. Lewis says, is "written all over the world" and changes the world for the better.

Questions about whether to go up or down in this world will almost certainly come up again and again in your life, even if you don't recognize what is happening.

For example, the following question could present itself to a couple with children:

Do we both go and get a job outside the home so that we can afford a nicer _____ (car, home, a better retirement), or will we live frugally on one income so we can spend more time with our children?

A hard-working father may ask:

Do I get a job or start a business that pays significantly more but requires me to be away so much that I miss my children growing up?

Am I willing to have fewer things now to give my children more of me, of my time, or will I trade that so they can just have more and better stuff?

Is physical stuff that is going to age, rapidly become outdated, rust, and decay really worth trading an opportunity to influence my children and their generations for thousands of years after I die?

The answer to these questions depends largely on whether or not, deep down, we believe that this world is all there is and if we are really aware of the Real World or not.

These deeply held beliefs are important to recognize and then ask if they are really true. I call them assumptions.

So much depends on the assumptions that we make about others, the world, and ourselves. Often we don't even realize that we have assumptions, as they are so deep-rooted and often not even something we really think about.

It is important that we find out and examine our assumptions so that we can see if they are real. If they are not true, we need to work hard to overcome them.

If we have the deep, even unspoken or unconscious, assumption that this world is all there is, then our decisions will be made on that assumption.

More importantly, we need to find out what is really, really real. What is true?

I don't want to believe something just because it will benefit society or my family or my religion. I want to believe something because it is *true*.

Stephen Covey wrote about beliefs and values that may or may not match up with what is actually true. Beliefs and values are like maps. The actual terrain of life is what is really, really real. Covey asks us to question whether the map we have matches up with the *real* terrain.[35]

Can you imagine trying to climb a mountain in the Himalayas when your map says it is a cornfield in Nebraska?

Your map may tell you it is safe to keep moving through what seems to be a flat field, when in real life you are stepping and falling off a dangerously high cliff. It is so important that our maps match the terrain.[36]

Many, if not most of the problems that we see in the world can be attributed to people trying to make sense out of life using a map that does not match up with the real terrain.

Consider these two differing beliefs, or "maps":

Map (belief system) #1:

· This world is all there is.

· We are just an accident in space and just a step above the monkey.

Actions that may come from having this underlying belief:

Work as hard as you can to get as much money, recognition, power, and prestige as possible. Or focus on fleeting pleasure—eat, drink, and be merry, for

---

[35] Covey, Stephen R., *The Seven Habits of Highly Effective People*, (Simon and Schuster, 1989), 23-24.

[36] Covey, *The Seven Habits*, 23-24.

tomorrow we die (an unfortunate adage woven into many philosophies and almost as old as written history).

This kind of thinking may lead us to believe that it doesn't matter if we lie, cheat, or steal because we are going to die anyway—if you can get away with it, do it. You may as well live a little—even if it is at others' expense.

Map (belief system) #2:

- This world is NOT it.
- In fact, it is "enemy-occupied territory",[37] and we are in a civil war with the devil and with division itself. Christ is asking me to give everything I can to love others and overcome the enemy and his division so that we can be united and be His. What I am becoming really, really matters to me and to others. My choices now will affect me, those I know and love, and even all of humanity a million, a billion, and a trillion years from now. Everyone I know and meet will be alive forever because of what Christ did. What I am doing now is important.

Actions that may come from having this underlying belief:

Work on myself now. Repent now. Be willing to focus on what really matters—relationships, parenting, family, and most importantly, following Christ, who overcame this world and is asking us to follow Him and His example so that we can overcome it too—and become like Him.

Which of the two beliefs is really, really real?

Which belief/value map is closer to the actual terrain?

---

[37] Lewis, *Mere Christianity*, 46. Also, it is important to remember that the enemy is NOT other people. All people are created by God, and we should NOT see them as enemies. If they are acting as enemies, we are under obligation from Jesus himself to pray for them and do our best to love them.

Getting our maps to line up with the actual terrain matters.

And it matters a lot.

Because it will affect not only our lives but the lives of others thousands of years from now and beyond. Please, my dear children, take the time to figure out what is really, really real.

> No one a few generations from now is going to care one iota about what you are doing for work today.

Please don't worship prestige or things or business and financial success by spending all your energy thinking you are climbing up when you are actually climbing down in a world turned on its head.

Consider how Paul in his epistle to the Philippians gives us a hint about how the world is upside down. God loves exalting humble servants of no reputation:

> Let this mind be in you, which was also in Christ Jesus: Who, being in the form of God, thought it not robbery to be equal with God: But made himself of no reputation, and took upon him the form of a servant, and was made in the likeness of men:[38]

> Generations from now, the kind of parent you were will mean infinitely more than what you did for work.

Notice how Jesus chose to go "down" the social ladder in our world by making himself of "no reputation" and "took upon him the form of a servant."

> And being found in fashion as a man, he humbled himself, and became obedient unto death, even the death of the cross.[39]

---

[38] Philippians 2:5–7.
[39] Philippians 2:8.

Notice that He both "humbled himself" and "became obedient unto death." Neither of these are something that is valued much in our inverted world.

> Wherefore God also hath highly exalted him, and given
> him a name which is above every name:[40]

Jesus humbling himself resulted in Him being exalted *above* "every name."

> That at the name of Jesus every knee should bow, of
> things in heaven, and things in earth, and things under
> the earth;
>
> And that every tongue should confess that Jesus Christ
> is Lord, to the glory of God the Father.[41]

Notice that God wants every knee to bow to the "servant" who made himself of "no reputation."

In the scripture above, Jesus, the God of the whole universe (who happened to be born in a stable and lived as a poor carpenter), chose to move "down" our capsized world's social ladder.

He was at the bottom of the world's social ladder but at the top of God's Real World.

To go down in this world is to go up in the Real World.

C.S. Lewis said:

> [Jesus] was not at all like the psychologist's picture of the
> integrated, balanced, adjusted, happily married,
> employed, popular citizen. You can't really be very well
> "adjusted" to your world if it says you "have a devil" and
> ends by nailing you up naked to a stake of wood.[42]

Yet this world places value on being integrated, balanced, employed, and popular, as well as well adjusted. Which begs a question:

---

[40] Philippians 2:9.

[41] Philippians 2:10–11.

[42] Lewis, C.S., *The Four Loves*, (Geoffrey Bles, 1960), 54.

How important is it to you to be "balanced" and "well adjusted" to living in the devil's enemy-occupied territory? Is that a goal we really should have?

Or is it better to be as Christ—telling the truth of the Real World, let the consequences come as they may?

Remember, God seems to often use people who others in this world perceive as being "at the bottom."

If you feel that what you are doing is low and not worthwhile, realize that the world is upside down and that "lowly" things, such as parenting, may be among the most valuable things you can do.

Do you really want to make a real difference? Become the best parent you can!

If you feel like you are at the bottom in this life, realize that God is likely preparing and using you for something more toward the top of His list.

And luckily, His list is in the Real World, and it is the list that really matters.

This World Is *Not* It

He that loveth his life shall lose it; and he that hateth his life in this world shall keep it unto life eternal.[43]

Peace I leave with you, my peace I give unto you: not as the world giveth, give I unto you. Let not your heart be troubled, neither let it be afraid.[44]

Chief among the problems we face are beliefs about ourselves and the world and the universe that simply are not true.

Unfortunately, many of the lies we believe are rooted in *deep* assumptions that are thought to be true, often by almost "everyone," when, in fact, they are not true.

These assumptions are everywhere and are often hidden.

In one of my university psychology classes, a great teacher by the name of Brent Slife was very skilled in teaching others how to find underlying assumptions.[45] For example, even science, which some see as completely objective, is not. It has underlying assumptions that are the premise for all of science. For example, in science, the unstated assumption is that if it is not measurable and observable, it is not

---

[43] John 12:25.
[44] John 14:27.
[45] Slife, B.D. and Williams, R.N., *What's Behind the Research?* (Sage, 1955)

important enough to study. However, God is usually neither overtly observable nor measurable by our limited five senses. Thus, from the perspective of this flawed assumption, God is not important enough to study.

An offshoot of this flawed assumption results in one of the biggest lies ever told:

This life is all there is. When we are dead, we are dead—so we should just make the most of it.

This lie has been told for millennia in different and subtle ways. The *current version* of this lie is weaved into what children are taught in school, into scientific literature/news articles, and into many other information sources. It goes something like this: The world and all life on it are simply the result of a cosmic accident. Humans are just hyper-evolved monkeys. Because of this, we should make the best of this life while we have it.

(Please note: I am deeply grateful for the wonderful contributions of scientists around the world. Their diligence and thoughtfulness has improved countless lives and I am grateful for the contributions they have made and continue to make. That said, it is still important to examine the assumptions that underpin the general scientific discipline.)

This thinking has been around for a long, long time. In the old, biblical days it was: "Eat, drink, and be merry, for tomorrow we die."

The underlying message is that you should do everything you can to make this life pleasurable, comfortable, and enjoyable, because, hey, we are just an accident, so why not enjoy it while it lasts?

The deeper, more sinister assumption in this lie that is rarely said but understood because of the nature of the lie is this:

Because everything is perceived as just an accident, the strong implication is that there is no absolute right or wrong and thus no good and evil—a lie built implicitly into the assumption, even if it is not explicitly stated. This insinuation that right and wrong don't exist, is insidious and, frankly, evil.

But we must look for truth, even if we don't like what we find.

C.S. Lewis said it best:

> If you look for truth, you may find comfort in the end: if you look for comfort you will not get either comfort or truth--only soft soap and wishful thinking to begin with and, in the end, despair.[46]

I believe that the truth is this (even though at the moment it could be seen as less than comforting):

> Enemy-occupied territory—that is what this world is. Christianity is the story of how the rightful king has landed, you might say landed in disguise, and is calling us all to take part in a great campaign of sabotage.[47]

It is important to remember that the enemy is NOT other people. All people are created by God, and we should NOT see them as enemies. If they are acting as enemies, we are under obligation, from Jesus Himself, to pray for them and do our best to love them.

The enemy is the devil and division itself—not our fellow human beings. We sabotage the system by believing in the truth—which is that all people are children of God—and by trying, like God, to see the mountains of good in them. We then choose to love others like Christ did. Christ asked the Father to forgive the very people who crucified Him and those who didn't believe in Him. We "sabotage" discord and division by being a peacemaker, loving our enemies and those different from us, blessing them that are rude to and curse us, and turning the other cheek.

Following Christ's commands, at least in the long run, creates unity, which, in turn, does indeed "sabotage" the division that exists in the world.

I believe that where there is spiritual misery, there is a lie somewhere.

Consider the following three examples:

- A man commits suicide when his life savings and investments are wiped out as the stock market falls sharply.

---

[46] Lewis, *Mere Christianity*, 32.

[47] Lewis, *Mere Christianity*, 46.

- A group of protesters, angry about current conditions, morphs into a violent mob, destroying lives and property as they rampage in a rage through a city.

- An angry spouse makes up false accusations to try to get more assets in a divorce proceeding.

All of these situations have in them a common assumption—an assumption that is a lie, often hidden beneath the surface.

The problem lies in the fact that people in the situations above seem to be acting as if this world is all there is.

And the belief that this world is all there is—it is a lie.

It is 100% false.

Let's examine the consequences that result from believing that this world is *it*.

Regarding the man who commits suicide over losing money:

Of course, if he has devoted his entire life to acquiring money and wealth, and *if he believes that this life is all there is*, it may make sense that having his wealth wiped out in a financial crisis would cause him to think of suicide as the only answer.

Indeed, in this situation, what he devoted his life to—acquiring wealth—is now gone. Also gone is all the time—the life, if you will—that he spent trying to get wealth.

He may have watched literally decades of his life go down the drain in a single stock market move.

The angry protestors are so riled up about whatever perceived injustice they are protesting that they are willing to turn violent. They are willing to risk both their own lives and the lives of others as a violent mob because of the underlying assumption that this life is all there is, and thus the injustice needs to be corrected *now*. They need it now, in this life.

The dishonest divorcing spouse is willing to lie to get what they feel they want now. They believe that they can make false accusations and get away with it, avoiding any consequences for dishonesty. They are willing to ruin others' lives and even possibly set a horrible example for their children because they want what they want in this life and are willing to make false accusations to get it. Why would they do that? Because, in their mind, this life is all there is, and so it seems worth it for them to lie to get what they want.

I understand this line of thinking. I "get" why people do it.

And yet I don't agree they should do it.

Almost every meaningful experience in my whole life seems to have built up to me sharing with you these two seemingly contradictory things:

1. Life is short and should be cherished.
2. It's not about this life.

Let me tell you why I believe this. For a moment, please imagine this:

Jesus is standing nobly and meekly in front of Pilate just before He is crucified.

My guess is that Pilate, on some level, can sense something undeniably different about Jesus.

In the back of his mind, he may remember that his wife warned him to do nothing harmful to Jesus, saying, "Have thou nothing to do with that just man: for I have suffered many things this day in a dream because of him."[48]

Pilate then begins to question Jesus, trying to get more of a sense as to why so many everywhere adore him and why many still want him dead.

At some point during their conversation, Jesus responds: "My Kingdom is not of this world: if my kingdom were of this world, then would my servants fight that I should not be delivered to the Jews: but now is my kingdom not from hence."[49]

Think of those words.

Jesus, probably very calmly, said, *"My Kingdom is not of this world."*

Let that marinate.

My. Kingdom. Is. Not. Of. This. World.

---

[48] Matthew 27:19.
[49] John 18:36.

Then, as if to make sure Pilate really got it, he said again, *"but now is my kingdom not from hence."*

This is Jesus, the Lord of the whole universe, saying that He could get out of this whole crucifixion thing, He could avoid dying a very painful death, and He could indeed have his servants fight and save Him from being crucified.

But He doesn't.

Why?

Jesus is letting both Pilate and us know that this world is *NOT* it.

Many who are convinced that this world is all there is may think: What? Is this Jesus crazy? Obviously, Jesus is not convinced that making this life comfortable and great is the thing to do. He is about to get crucified. He knows it. He knows He could stop it. Yet He doesn't. What?

Now, for those of you reading this book who may not believe in Jesus, I need to take a quick break, as the words above may not hold much weight with you.

For the moment, I don't need you to believe in Jesus, but I do want you to consider a few thoughts from C.S. Lewis:

> Christianity . . . if false, is of no importance, and, if true,
> of infinite importance. The only thing it cannot be is
> moderately important.[50]

No middle ground—Christianity either matters immensely, or it doesn't matter at all.

Next, I feel I need to include below C.S. Lewis's reply to the currently somewhat popular notion that Jesus Christ was a great moral teacher, but not God:

> I am trying here to prevent anyone saying the really
> foolish thing that people often say about Him: 'I'm ready
> to accept Jesus as a great moral teacher, but I don't
> accept His claim to be God.' That is the one thing we

---

[50] Lewis, C.S., *God in the Dock*, (Eerdmans, 1970), 101.

must not say. A man who was merely a man and said the sort of things Jesus said would not be a great moral teacher. He would either be a lunatic—on a level with the man who says he is a poached egg—or else he would be the Devil of Hell. You must make your choice. Either this man was, and is, the Son of God: or else a madman or something worse. You can shut Him up for a fool, you can spit at Him and kill Him as a demon; or you can fall at His feet and call Him Lord and God, but let us not come with any patronising nonsense about His being a great human teacher. He has not left that open to us. He did not intend to.[51]

Just ponder that quote for a minute or two.

Let it sink in, then let's continue.

Pilate, almost certainly still sensing something a bit different about this Jesus, continues questioning him:

Pilate therefore said unto him, Art thou a king then? Jesus answered, Thou sayest I am a king. To this end was I born, and for this cause came I into the world, that I should bear witness unto the truth. *Every one that is of the truth heareth my voice.*[52]

Two points are important here:

1. Jesus says, "for this cause came I into the world," which strongly implies that He came from somewhere outside of the world. Of course, this is repetitive, as He has already let Pilate know more than once that His kingdom is not of this world. Jesus knows that the world we are in is not all there is.

2. Jesus says that He is here to simply tell the truth and that every one that is "of the truth" hears His voice.

---

[51] Lewis, *Mere Christianity*, 52.
[52] John 18:37, emphasis added.

Now, if in any way the words you just read "hit" you somehow (even a little bit), or if Jesus's words at any time have been impressed upon your mind—are you open to the possibility that you are one of the people that Jesus says is "of the truth"?

Whether you are "of the truth" or not is a big deal.

A really big deal.

It means more than you may think.

Let's contrast the enemy's propaganda with what Jesus said:

Enemy Propaganda: Since this world is all there is, I should do all I can to make myself go upward in it. If I am great, people should serve me. I can achieve greatness by becoming wealthy, famous, or by achieving something "great." With my achievements, wealth, and fame, I should expect others to serve me—I can hire employees, servants, or others to take care of my needs. I can live a life of luxury and ease.

Jesus Himself: "But he that is greatest among you shall be your servant. And whosoever shall exalt himself shall be abased; and he that shall humble himself shall be exalted."[53]

Do you see the difference? The enemy says one thing, Jesus says exactly the opposite. The enemy's words sound good and appealing to the "natural man" part of us, because they help us get what we want right now. Jesus' words don't sound as good to the "natural man" part of us because it reminds us of the truth—this world isn't it.

Christ shows up in this world. He is the real King. He is calling on us to follow Him—to take part in a "great campaign" of sabotaging not people, but division and hate. He reminds us that if we exalt ourselves in this world, we will be humbled when we reach the Real World.

But just how, exactly, do we follow Jesus?

By following His actual words (by the way, I didn't say by following the words of myself, some preacher, or someone who thinks they know—I said by following the words of the Master Himself).

So, for the man considering committing suicide when his wealth is wiped out, he could remember the words of the Jesus:

---

[53] Matthew 23:11–12.

> Lay not up for yourselves treasures upon earth, where moth and rust doth corrupt, and where thieves break through and steal: But lay up for yourselves treasures in heaven, where neither moth nor rust doth corrupt, and where thieves do not break through nor steal: For where your treasure is, there will your heart be also.[54]

For those in the angry mob, it would be wise to remember the actual words of the Jesus Himself:

> But I say unto you, Love your enemies, bless them that curse you, do good to them that hate you, and pray for them which despitefully use you, and persecute you; That ye may be the children of your Father which is in heaven: for he maketh his sun to rise on the evil and on the good, and sendeth rain on the just and on the unjust.[55]

> Ye have heard that it was said of them of old time, Thou shalt not kill; and whosoever shall kill shall be in danger of the judgment: But I say unto you, That whosoever is angry with his brother without a cause shall be in danger of the judgment: and whosoever shall say to his brother, Raca, shall be in danger of the council: but whosoever shall say, Thou fool, shall be in danger of hell fire.[56]

For the dishonest divorcing spouse, it may be well to remember these words of Jesus:

> But I say unto you, That every idle word that men shall speak, they shall give account thereof in the day of judgment.[57]

---

[54] Matthew 6:19–21.

[55] Matthew 5:44–45.

[56] Matthew 5:21–22.

[57] Matthew 12:36.

Notice that the answers to each situation are given by the True King, in Jesus's own words.

If this world is not it, why, then, do we often act and even fight to climb the social ladder as if this world is all there is?

Why do we neglect our loved ones, spend more time with business associates than our own children and loved ones, "fight" to have the best-looking house or car or something so that we can build kingdoms in this world, when this is *not* the kingdom that really matters?

Why do some fathers and mothers spend so much time working but almost no time building relationships with the ones they can influence most—their own children?

Is it so we can have more stuff? More prosperity? To exalt our station in this life?

Did you ever think that climbing the corporate ladder, or achieving more wealth, fame, or authority may possibly be getting you a better spot in the enemy's territory?

C.S. Lewis reminded us: "Aim at Heaven and you will get Earth 'thrown in': aim at Earth and you will get neither."[58]

Do you want to make a difference? Do you want to leave a legacy?

Remember that this world is not it.

And then do everything you can to follow Jesus.

---

[58] Lewis, *Mere Christianity*, 134.

Pattern of the King

Interestingly, Jesus Christ didn't show up with a slew of armies.

He didn't show up with a security detail or with an entourage or a film crew. He wasn't worried about how many followers he had on social media.

He didn't show up with gunfire, cannon fire, an explosion, or even lightning or thunder.

He showed up as a baby in a stable—a place where animals eat and defecate and sleep.

He was laid in the actual place the animals eat from—a manger, surrounded by a poor carpenter and a humble virgin.

This is important because it shows us the pattern that the Rightful King, Jesus, uses when He wants to get something done.

Small and simple things often go unnoticed in enemy-occupied territory.

When God wants to change something, He doesn't send an army, He sends a baby—in an animal-feeding trough.

When God wants to change the world, He often uses people who are small and simple and who no one would guess—people who are "low on the totem pole." He often uses people who are not popular, not polished. If you are feeling low and like you don't measure up, God may just be preparing you for something He needs you to do.

Do you feel you are not measuring up?

Do you feel that you need to be more popular?

More rich?

More famous?

When these feelings come, realize that if you want to "go up" in the Real World, be willing to do that which seems lowly in this world. Jesus washed men's feet. Jesus spent His time with the downtrodden, the poor, the sick, and the despised.

Why?

The world is upside down.

Principles

We can choose to do anything we want, but we do not control the consequences of our choices.

Principles control the consequences.

Our choices matter.

> You are the bows from which your children as living arrows are sent forth.
>
> The archer sees the make upon the path of the infinite, and He bends you with His might that His arrows may go swift and far.[59]

You may ask, "What should I teach my children?"

This may be one of the most important questions you could ever ask yourself.

Our children will likely be sent to a time we cannot see. We want our children to be strong, to be capable, to be arrows that "may go swift and far."

But here is the problem. For this to work, we have got to teach our children how things really, really are. To use Stephen Covey's analogy[60],

---

59 Gibran, Kahlil, "On Children."
60 Covey, *The Seven Habits*, 23-24.

our "map" and our terrain need to match as much as possible. And for that to happen, we first have to have a map that matches, as much as possible, the terrain. Otherwise, we will be handing our children a map that is false, that does not match the actual terrain. Imagine handing your children a map of Paris when they are trying to navigate the Grand Canyon. It wouldn't help them. It may even hurt them, as the map of Paris won't alert them to where the dangerous cliffs of the Grand Canyon are.

Our children will be blessed to the extent that we can give them a map that matches up with the real terrain.

Thus, we have to be brave and take an honest, real look at things. We may or may not like what we see, but whether we like it or not is beside the point. We need to know what is accurate—for both ourselves and our children's sake.

One of the things I believe is true whether anyone else believes it or not is that Jesus Christ was the literal Son of God, that He died for our sins, and that in doing so, He made it possible for us to return to God.

Remember the quote from C.S. Lewis:

> Christianity . . . if false, is of no importance, and, if true, of infinite importance. The only thing it cannot be is moderately important.[61]

C.S. Lewis is brilliant in describing why he believes Christianity is really, really real.

At this point, I recommend you stop and read C.S. Lewis's entire book *Mere Christianity.*

Please—just stop and read and consider the whole book before going on. It is not a very long book, but it is very valuable.

---

[61] Lewis, *God in the Dock*, 101.

If we take an honest look at the world, we notice that there are some things that are *just there*, whether we like them, or believe in them, or not. While some of these things change, some of these things are constant and don't change. We did not invent these. They are *just there*.

The things that don't change are called principles. And figuring out what they are, then teaching them to our children, is one of the best things we could ever do.

Principles cannot be invented. They are fundamental foundational truths. I can't invent them. You can't invent them. They are ancient. They are timeless.

Again, they are *just there*—whether you believe in them or not.

To illustrate, take the scientific *principle* of gravity. I didn't invent it. You didn't invent it. It has been around a really, really long time. And it is just *there*, even if you and I don't believe it.

In fact, gravity is more than just *there*. *It is everywhere.*

It keeps you and me on the ground.

It keeps the moon revolving around the earth.

It keeps the earth revolving around the sun.

In space, billions of miles away, there are clusters of galaxies spinning around, held together by gravity.

It's everywhere.

Let me clarify, I am not talking about principles in the way that many often use the word.

You've likely at some time heard something like this: "I have my principles and you have yours. My principles work for me, and your principles work for you."

Those are not the kinds of "principles" I am talking about.

In fact, the example above is more an example of values. It *is* possible to value different things. It is *not* possible to invent a principle, no matter what you value. Again, to use Stephen Covey's analogy, principles are the terrain, while values are the map we have in our head.

Problems happen when the "map" of our values doesn't match up with the actual terrain of real principles.

Can you imagine someone saying, "Gravity doesn't really work for me. It may work for you, but I don't need your old-fashioned beliefs about gravity!" That same person could jump off a cliff, really believing that they can fly, and they would fall, with devastating consequences.

In this book, when I use the word "principles," I am talking about principles that are *just as real and just as everywhere as gravity.*

Again, principles are really, really, really REAL—whether you believe in them or not.

Real truth really does exist, even if some doubt it.

I am talking about the terrain (principles), not the map (values).

Now, you have at least two choices when you encounter a principle: 1) align with it, or 2) ignore it—to your peril.

For example, with the principle of gravity—you can align with and respect it, and build a hydroelectric dam, start a skydiving company, build a ski resort, start a bungee-jumping business, build roller coasters, etc.

In fact, aligning with gravity might make you rich. The businesses above, and ones like it, have made many people rich—all by aligning with, and respecting, the principle of gravity. And if we spent more time, I think we could come up with dozens of different ways to align with gravity.

Or you can ignore gravity, to your peril, and not give it the respect it deserves and fall off a cliff, which could injure or even kill you.

So, gravity could make you rich, or gravity could kill you.

What makes the difference?

Gravity itself doesn't change.

The only thing that changes is your choice to either respect gravity and align with it or ignore gravity and/or be careless with it.

Align or ignore.

These are our choices when it comes to principles.

And that is all we really can choose.

Principles control the consequences—not us.

You can climb to the top of a cliff and think, "I believe I can fly!" You can really value the thought of jumping off a cliff and flying. But

84

once you jump off the cliff, the principle of gravity takes over, despite your belief and what you value.

It is therefore of utmost importance to find out exactly what the real principles are—the big stuff—which are bigger than you and me.

There are spiritual and human relations principles that are just as real as gravity.

Like gravity, spiritual and human relations principles are ancient and timeless.

What are these principles?

More about Principles

*He that hath my commandments, and keepeth them, he it is that
loveth me: and he that loveth me shall be loved of my Father, and
I will love him, and will manifest myself to him.*[62]

Principles are ancient and timeless.

They are larger than life—bigger, if you will, than you and me. We are NOT principles unto ourselves. We are subject to them, and they directly control the consequences of our choices, regardless of what we value. This is why it is so important to find out what they *actually* are.

Again, we can choose to do anything we want, but we do *not* control the consequences of our choices—principles do.

In many of my presentations, I teach people to try and find out what the principles in life *really* are—*the principles that govern everything.*

What are they <u>really</u>?

Here are some hints:

They aren't the latest fad.

They aren't the latest coaching program or book.

They aren't the newest *something*.

Principles are ancient and timeless.

Principles don't change.

---

[62] John 14:21.

They are there and will always be there.

The sooner we recognize and align with them, the sooner we can get to where we really want to be.

Let me illustrate:

I was flying on a large commercial airplane recently.

As I looked out the window, it occurred to me how amazing it is that an airplane (which I estimated probably weighs as much as fifty trucks) could fly tens of thousands of feet in the air. And it can do it for hours and hours with precision—it can transverse continents and oceans.

Now, I teach people to try and find out what the real principles are that govern everything, and so it occurred to me that I should practice what I preach.

I found that there is more than one principle that keeps a plane thousands of feet in the air, but chief among them is Bernoulli's principle.

Bernoulli's principle, as applied to aircraft, can be summed up like this: the wing is shaped so that, when planes move quickly, the air has to travel faster over the top than the bottom.

This "thins" the air above the wing and creates a low pressure. Low pressure is the same thing that causes liquid to move up a straw. So it is almost like there are big straws above the plane's wings, "sucking" the plane up.

That's it.

People can fly all over the globe because engineers have learned how to align with (and not ignore) Bernoulli's principle.

Now, here is my next question:

How long has Bernoulli's principle been around?

The answer:

Since the dawn of time.

When did we figure it out?

Sometime in the last several hundred years.

In other words, if man had figured out the principle before then, they might have been able to fly—but they didn't. We literally, on a historical level, have just barely figured it out. It would have been nice to have figured it out earlier, but we didn't—and yet the principle has existed literally since the dawn of time.

Spiritual principles are just as real.

Human relations principles are just as real.

Principles that will help you feel peace, that will help your marriage, and that will help a troubled teen are just as real.

But what are these principles?

We can spend our whole life looking for them.

Or we can learn quickly from the words of Jesus Christ.

Want a crash course on principles? There are strong hints about them in scripture. For example, Christ tells us all about the higher spiritual principles in His Sermon on the Mount (Matthew 5–7 in the Bible) and in his other sermons (see Matthew 10, 13, 18, and 23–25).

The Book of Galatians gives us some of these principles as well:

> But the fruit of the Spirit is love, joy, peace, longsuffering, gentleness, goodness, faith, meekness, temperance: against such there is no law.[63]

Warning: Aligning with the principles from the Sermon on the Mount will likely be very difficult.

Aligning with Bernoulli's principle was likely difficult as well. It was thousands of years before we finally "got" it, yet aligning with it takes planes higher and gives us freedom to travel. Similarly, the spiritual principles found in the Sermon on the Mount can take us higher spiritually and give us spiritual freedom to go places not possible before.

---

[63] Galatians 5:22–23.

Free Will and Real Love

Free will is the *Sanctum Sanctorum* (Latin meaning Holy of Holies) of principles. It's the big stuff – the stuff you can't mess with. God considers this so important that He won't take it away. We get to make our own choices.

In the Real World, having real Christlike love is everything. It is the only thing that really matters. Getting it is everything.

Free will and real love are inseparably connected. They are part of each other.

Free will acknowledges that we cannot always choose our circumstances, but we can always choose the attitude of how we respond to those circumstances. In other words, we don't control the external environment, but we *can* choose how we respond to it, including how we respond to the people around us.

Unlike objects, which are completely subject to laws and principles such as gravity, we literally have something no object has—the gift of free will—the ability to choose. This principle interacts with all other principles and is, at the same time, supreme over all the other principles.

We always have a choice—always. We can lessen our ability to choose through breaking the commandments, poor choices, addiction, and so on, but we still have a choice.

91

Thus, when one person is trying to influence another, the influencer can do everything "right" by aligning with real human relations principles, and the person they are trying to influence can still resist and say "no." We can say yes to good things and to bad things. We can say no to bad things as well as good things. And we can do it regardless of how good the person influencing us is at influencing.

This means that no matter how much pressure people put on us to do something, we can still say no.

This means that no matter how much pressure people put on us to *not* do something, we can still say yes and do it anyway.

This applies to all people—and God, in His humility, even made it so that we can say "no" to Him if we choose.

Why would God, who is all-powerful, give us the ability to tell even Him "no"? Why wouldn't an all-powerful God just force us to do His will?

In *Mere Christianity*, C.S. Lewis explains:

> . . . free will, though it makes evil possible, is also the only thing that makes possible any love or goodness or joy worth having.
>
> Of course God knew what would happen if they used their freedom the wrong way: apparently He thought it worth the risk.[64]

In other words, to have God's unbelievable love and joy, we need to be *free*.

So, it is not surprising, that in our world we find that many misguided assumptions have infiltrated science, therapy, and psychology. Here is an example of an underlying assumption that is misguided, or more frankly, a lie:

We are simply a mixture of our nature and nurture. We cannot determine what DNA and genes we are born with—this is referred to by some as our "nature." Nor can we change how we were raised—

---

[64] Lewis, *Mere Christianity*, 48.

referred to by some as our "nurture." This combination of what has happened to us (our past, or "nurture") combined with the genes we were born with (our "nature") determines our future.

There are some who adamantly argue that free will does not even exist, that humans are simply a complex product of nature and nurture, and this is a belief that is becoming more common, though less often overtly spoken.

Some people are even given diagnoses by professional therapists that leave them with the message that their disorder is permanent—that's just unfortunately the way they are, due to nature and nurture. The assumption is that my past and my heredity, or chance, somehow determine my present and future. It is a belief that seems to be more and more common.

But is it true?

Do my past, my heredity, or chance really determine my present and future?

Absolutely not.

This is truth mixed with lie. The truth is that our past does affect our present, but it does *not* determine it.

The "determine" part is the lie.

Of course our past can really, really affect us, but it does *not* determine our future. God gave us free will, and because of that, we are able to overcome and transcend the scripts and the baggage, the hurt and pain of the past.

It does not mean that overcoming it will be easy. It may take an immense amount of work and God's grace to do it. But we can overcome and transcend our past—the mistakes of others as well as our own mistakes—with God's help.

I need to say it again: Our past does *not* determine our present or our future.

We can transcend. We can overcome.

We are given power when we

1. are humble enough to realize that we are not a principle unto ourselves.

2. really search out what the true principles are.

3. make our daily tiny decisions align with real principles—and better yet, align with the Creator Himself, Jesus Christ.

God, who created us--created us with free will—now asks us to do something terrifying.

He asks us to give our free will, our ability to choose, back to Him.

To many, the thought of giving up their will sounds almost like voluntarily becoming a slave.

But something amazing happens when we give up our will to follow Jesus. Instead of being enslaved, our freedom increases. Our ability to choose increases. Our ability to love increases. It seems absolutely counterintuitive, even backward, but in this one principle is hidden probably the biggest treasure of the Real World.

Then again, Jesus told us about hidden treasures:

> Again, the kingdom of heaven is like unto treasure hid in a field; the which when a man hath found, he hideth, and for joy thereof goeth and selleth all that he hath, and buyeth that field.[65]

Note that he did NOT say the kingdom of God is like a lighthouse that can be seen from anywhere—just look around and you will be sure to see it. He said it is like a treasure *hidden* in a field.

The kingdom of God is hidden in exactly this principle: When we let our will get swallowed up in Christ, we learn to truly love. Really, really love—like Christ did.

The reason it is hidden is this: to many, the thought of giving up their will to Christ sounds almost like death.

But it's not.

It's more like aligning with gravity and building a hydroelectric dam that makes you millions of dollars a year. When you align with Jesus Christ Himself, you start to become as He is: full of unstoppable, unspeakable Christlike love.

---

[65] Matthew 13:44.

When we try with all our might to follow Christ's words—to love our enemies, to bless them that curse us, to turn the other cheek, to cast the mote out of our own eye, etc., *big* stuff starts to happen.

Neal A. Maxwell said this:

> In conclusion, the submission of one's will is really the only uniquely personal thing we have to place on God's altar. The many other things we "give," brothers and sisters, are actually the things He has already given or loaned to us. However, when you and I finally submit ourselves, by letting our individual wills be swallowed up in God's will, then we are really giving something to Him! It is the only possession which is truly ours to give!
>
> Consecration thus constitutes the only unconditional surrender, which is also a total victory![66]

Ironically, surrendering our will to God is exactly what gives us the victory and hidden treasure of the Real World.

God will never force us to join Him. He waits patiently and *humbly* for us to come to ourselves.

To quote C.S. Lewis:

> I call this a Divine humility because it is a poor thing to strike our colours to God when the ship is going down under us . . . If God were proud He would hardly have us on such terms: but He is not proud, He stoops to conquer, He will have us even though we have shown that we prefer everything else to Him, and come to Him because there is 'nothing better' now to be had.[67]

And he also reminds us:

> God cannot give us a happiness and peace apart from Himself, because it is not there. There is no such thing.[68]

---

[66] Maxwell, Neal A., "Swallowed Up in the Will of the Father." (1995)

[67] Lewis, C.S., *The Problem of Pain*, (The Centenary Press, 1940), 62.

[68] Lewis, *Mere Christianity*, 50.

It may sound weird that surrendering your choices to Christ will actually give you more power and, well, choices. Most importantly, though, it will teach you to have Christlike love—the main thing.

But then again, most hidden treasures probably sound a bit weird the first time you hear about them.

And learning to have Christlike love is the biggest treasure of all.

Love Is the Answer

True Christlike love is the answer. There are different kinds of love. Christlike love is superior love, and it helps and causes to flourish all the other kinds of love.[69] It is the kind of unconditional, transformative love that Christ has for us. People who possess, or I might say, are possessed of, this kind of love are not concerned about reciprocity, or getting what they "deserve." People with this kind of love give even when others don't deserve it—just like Christ died for us when we didn't deserve it.

Sometimes scripture refers to this superior Christlike kind of love as charity. Having it is everything. If you don't have it, you are nothing in the Real World.

> Though I speak with the tongues of men and of angels, and have not charity, I am become as sounding brass, or a tinkling cymbal. And though I have the gift of prophecy, and understand all mysteries, and all knowledge; and though I have all faith, so that I could remove mountains, and have not charity, I am nothing. And though I bestow all my goods to feed the poor, and though I give my body to be burned, and have not charity, it profiteth me nothing.[70]

---

[69] Lewis, *The Four Loves.*
[70] 1 Corinthians 13:1–3.

True Christlike love is everything. It doesn't matter what else you have if you don't have this at the last day. Do everything you can to get it. Pray for it like it is the only thing that matters—because in the Real World, it is.

> Wherefore, my beloved brethren, pray unto the Father with all the energy of heart, that ye may be filled with this love, which he hath bestowed upon all who are true followers of his Son, Jesus Christ; that ye may become the sons of God.[71]

This may sound quaint, humorous, or even offensive to some people, but the truth is that "Love Is the Answer."

To everything.

But what if you don't feel love for someone?

1. Pray to have Christ's love with all your heart.
2. Lead your feelings with actions.

---

[71] Moroni 7:48.

We Lead Our Feelings with Our Actions

The world has it backward. The world teaches that we should do whatever our feelings tell us to do—just follow our feelings.

Here's the problem: have you ever noticed that your feelings are like the weather? You can be laughing one moment and angry the next, and then embarrassed the next. If you base your choices on your feelings, your results will be unpredictable and fickle, just like the weather.

In Stephen Covey's book *The Seven Habits of Highly Effective People*, he writes the following:

> "At one seminar where I was speaking on the concept of proactivity, a man came up and said, 'Stephen, I like what you're saying. But every situation is so different. Look at my marriage. I'm really worried. My wife and I just don't have the same feelings for each other we used to have. I guess I just don't love her anymore and she doesn't love me. What can I do?'
>
> 'The feeling isn't there anymore?' I asked.
>
> 'That's right,' he reaffirmed. 'And we have three children we're really concerned about. What do you suggest?'
>
> 'Love her,' I replied.

'I told you, the feeling just isn't there anymore.'

'Love her.'

'You don't understand. The feeling of love just isn't there.'

'Then love her. If the feeling isn't there, that's a good reason to love her.'

'But how do you love when you don't love?'

'My friend, love is a verb. Love—the feeling—is a fruit of love, the verb. So love her. Serve her. Sacrifice. Listen to her. Empathize. Appreciate. Affirm her. Are you willing to do that?'

In the great literature of all progressive societies, love is a verb. Reactive people make it a feeling. They're driven by feelings. Hollywood has generally scripted us to believe that we are not responsible, that we are a product of our feelings. But the Hollywood script does not describe the reality. If our feelings control our actions, it is because we abdicated our responsibility and empowered them to do so."[72]

Side note: It is imperative that we become aware of the influence that the media and Hollywood have on our scripts and how we see the world.

Covey continues:

"Proactive people make love a verb. Love is something you do: the sacrifice you make, the giving of self, like a mother bringing a newborn into the world. If you want to study love, study those who sacrifice for others, even for people who offend or do not love in return. If you are a parent, look at the love you have for the children you sacrificed for. Love is a value that is actualized

---

[72] Covey, *The Seven Habits*, 79-80.

through loving actions. Proactive people subordinate feelings to values. Love, the feeling, can be recaptured."[73]

It's not just the feeling of love that we can lead with our actions.

I remember talking with a friend of mine who committed himself to a very physically demanding workout.

He said that the first time he did the workout, it made his muscles very sore, as it was a very intense workout.

Despite the intensity of the soreness, he decided to keep doing the workout repeatedly.

Each day after finishing the workout, he was so sore he "wanted to die."

He hated it but kept doing it, day after day, for weeks.

Then it happened. What he said next was interesting:

"Somewhere around week two and a half or three, something changed. I got to the end of the workout, and instead of being so sore that I wanted to die, *for the first time, I felt like I was just getting started. I wanted to do the workout again*, and so I did.

"It happened again the next day. I got to the end of the workout, and I wanted to do it again, so I did."

You see, he led his feelings. He exercised before he felt like it, and it took two and a half to three weeks for his feelings to catch up with his actions.

But his feelings did indeed follow his actions, and after a while, he felt like doing the workout.

Leading your feelings works. Waiting for a feeling to come along before you take action almost never works. Can you imagine saying, "I'm just going to sit here on the couch and do nothing until I feel like exercising"? It won't work.

The truth is, you have to exercise for two or three weeks, and then the feeling can follow!

But where? Where should you lead them?

Here are some hints:

---

[73] Covey, *The Seven Habits*, 80.

1. Admit that you are not a principle unto yourself.

2. Figure out what the real principles really, really are.

3. Make your little, tiny daily decisions align with timeless principles.

That's it.

If you can get to the point where you lead your feelings with your actions and take responsibility for your own feelings, you will be on the road to getting what matters most.

Lead.

Your.

Feelings.

With.

Actions.

To.

Love.

Others.

If you pray to love as Christ loves with everything you have, and then act by trusting Him enough to give your will to Him—by really loving others, you will start to love others as Christ does.

> Instead of letting your feelings lead you, choose to lead your feelings.

This love is *unstoppable* in the Real World, because as Paul the Apostle made clear: *Charity never faileth.*[74]

Charity—the true love of Christ—*never* fails—ever. It is the big stuff. It is the only stuff

---

[74] 1 Corinthians 13:8, emphasis added.

that matters in the Real World. We get it by giving our free will to Christ, who in turn makes us into something more than we can imagine.

The Most Important Thing to

Remember When Teaching Others

There are three things that are important when teaching others:

1) example
2) example
3) example

Example is the most important thing. However, sometimes we as parents say to do one thing and then do another ourselves. I know that I am guilty of this.

In Matthew 23, it reads:

> Then spake Jesus to the multitude, and to his disciples, Saying The scribes and the Pharisees sit in Moses' seat: All therefore whatsoever they bid you observe, that observe and do; *but do not ye after their works: for they say, and do not.* For they bind heavy burdens and grievous to be borne, and lay them on men's shoulders; but they themselves will not move them with one of their fingers. But all their works they do for to be seen of men.[75]

---

[75] Matthew 23:1–5, emphasis added.

Later in the same sermon:

> Woe unto you, scribes and Pharisees, hypocrites! for ye pay tithe of mint and anise and cummin, and have omitted the weightier matters of the law, judgment, mercy, and faith: these ought ye to have done, and not to leave the other undone. Ye blind guides, which strain at a gnat, and swallow a camel. Woe unto you, scribes and Pharisees, hypocrites! for ye make clean the outside of the cup and of the platter, but within they are full of extortion and excess. Thou blind Pharisee, cleanse first that which is within the cup and platter, that the outside of them may be clean also. Woe unto you, scribes and Pharisees, hypocrites! for ye are like unto whited sepulchres, which indeed appear beautiful outward, but are within full of dead men's bones, and of all uncleanness. Even so ye also outwardly appear righteous unto men, but within ye are full of hypocrisy and iniquity.[76]

Christ's most intense words were against hypocrites.

In Luke 18, Christ makes very clear how important it is to admit to ourselves and others that we are sinners.

> And he spake this parable unto certain which trusted in themselves that they were righteous, and despised others:[77]

If there is anyone you despise, that is a signal that you need to pray to love that person. It doesn't matter if it is a politician you don't like, someone who has really hurt you, or anyone else. Pray for that person. Pray for your ability to have charity for that person. Pray that you can love them as Jesus did. Per Jesus Himself, if we feel we are despising someone, we need to stop and pray for them.

---

[76] Matthew 23:23–28.
[77] Luke 18:9.

Also, if we feel and "trust" that we are righteous, we are in a really dangerous spot. Remember, it is okay, even honest, to admit you are a sinner.

> Two men went up into the temple to pray; the one a Pharisee, and the other a publican. The Pharisee stood and prayed thus with himself, God, I thank thee, that I am not as other men are, extortioners, unjust, adulterers, or even as this publican. I fast twice in the week, I give tithes of all that I possess. And the publican, standing afar off, would not lift up so much as his eyes unto heaven, but smote upon his breast, saying, God be merciful to me a sinner. I tell you, this man went down to his house justified rather than the other: for every one that exalteth himself shall be abased; and he that humbleth himself shall be exalted.[78]

I am a sinner. Worse, I am and have been a hypocrite. I try to do what I preach but fall short much of the time. I need a Savior and am trying to repent. I ask for Jesus to be that Savior. I hope to do my best to repent.

---

[78] Luke 18:10–14.

The Importance of Family

As a dad, I have a divine responsibility to do the three Ps for my family: preside, provide, and protect.

To preside means that I have the responsibility to love, to teach my children the Word of God, and to be the spiritual leader in my home. A father should take the initiative to make sure that the family attends church, has regular family scripture study, makes time for spiritual things, and spends time together as a family. A father should not abdicate this responsibility to anyone else.

As a father, it is also my duty to provide diligently for the needs of my family.

It is not the duty of the state, the school, the church, or any other program.

It is my duty to provide.

In times of hardship, any temporary assistance from outside sources should be just that—temporary.

It is also my job as a father to protect my family, both spiritually and physically.

My wife has the primary responsibility to nurture.

Though our responsibilities are different, we are equal partners.

Gods in Embryo versus Things

People are gods in embryo, just like you.
They are *not* things; they are *not* objects.
Treat them as they are—like gods in embryo.

When I Discuss God with Friends

When I discuss things with friends who don't believe in God, I am often asked by them to think about things in a different way. They ask me to consider what is true and what is false and what can be considered facts.

All of these conversations take for granted, or assume, something.

It is assumed by my friends that we can trust our own brain, that "considering" and "thinking" have some value, that focusing this brain may, in fact, lead us to the facts.

That said, consider this comment by C.S. Lewis:

> Supposing there was no intelligence behind the universe, no creative mind. In that case, nobody designed my brain for the purpose of thinking. It is merely that when the atoms inside my skull happen, for physical or chemical reasons, to arrange themselves in a certain way, this gives me, as a by-product, the sensation I call thought. But, if so, how can I trust my own thinking to be true? It's like upsetting a milk jug and hoping that the way it splashes itself will give you a map of London. But if I can't trust my own thinking, of course I can't trust the arguments leading to Atheism, and therefore have no reason to be an Atheist, or anything else. *Unless I believe*

in God, I cannot believe in thought: so I can never use thought to disbelieve in God.[79]

Now, let that marinate.

I have found that often people choose not to believe in God because the universe seems so unfair. It seems cruel. They ask, "If there is a God, why is there so much pain?" It seems to them that much of the universe *should* or *should not* be a certain way.

Consider this quote from C.S. Lewis:

> If a good God made the world why has it gone wrong? And for many years I simply refused to listen to the Christian answers to this question . . .
>
> My argument against God was that the universe seemed so cruel and unjust. But how had I got this idea of *just* and *unjust?* A man does not call a line crooked unless he has some idea of a straight line. What was I comparing this universe with when I had called it unjust? *If the whole show was bad and senseless from A to Z, so to speak, why did I, who was supposed to be part of the show, find myself in such violent reaction against it?* . . . Of course I could have given up my idea of justice by saying it was nothing but a private idea of my own. But if I did that, then my argument against God collapsed too—*for the argument depended on saying that the world was really unjust, not simply that it did not happen to please my fancies.*[80]

Either our ideas of what is fair or not are full of sense, *or* they are just an accident based on what evolution has caused us to privately fancy.

Which is it?

For my friends who don't believe in God, is it possible that we don't fully belong to the show? That some part of us knows what a show *should*

---

[79] Lewis, C.S., *The Case for Christianity*, (The MacMillan Company, 1943), 32, emphasis added.

[80] Lewis, *Mere Christianity*, 38-39, emphasis added.

look like, and you and I find ourselves in this show and know that parts of it are not as they *should* be?

Turn the Other Cheek

In Matthew 5:39, the Savior teaches a higher principle. It is a principle that I believe the Savior knew was so important, He said:

> But I say unto you, That ye resist not evil: but whosoever shall smite thee on thy right cheek, turn to him the other also.[81]

For a brief but very clear moment in the autumn of 2021, while I was pondering, I had an understanding come to me that I hadn't before. Without specific words coming to mind, for just a few moments I felt I could understand the "turn the other cheek" principle of the gospel as I never had before. I could comprehend how important it is to just do the right thing, especially when others don't. When we perceive injustice, there is a natural tendency to "hit back." I now somehow knew why we should not.

I quickly rushed to find something to write with and then struggled to put into words what I had just experienced.

When we turn the other cheek, we are essentially saying, "I believe in the good in you. I will not stop believing in your good, even if you hit me. I have faith that the good and Godlike part of you will come through, even if it takes a very long time."

---

81 Matthew 5:39.

In the movie *Gandhi*, the character Gandhi said something like this: "... you must show courage; be willing to take a blow, several blows, to show you will not strike back nor will you be turned aside. And when you do that, it calls on something in human nature—something that makes his hatred for you decrease and his respect increase. I think Christ grasped that, and I have seen it work."[82]

This concept starts with something a wise counselor and mentor told me, which I didn't really get at first, but which came to me again during this recent experience.

His words were profound and went something like this: "Eks, when somebody does something wrong, you don't have to point it out to them. That is the job of the Light of Christ. Trust the Light of Christ."

The Light of Christ is the power given to every single person in the world to distinguish between good and evil. Conscience—the ability to know and feel what is right and wrong—is part of the Light of Christ.

This light is "given to every man,"[83] which light of Christ will, indeed, teach us "all things what [we] should do."[84]

In other words:

Everybody has it.

And it can teach me and everybody else everything we need to do.

I can trust, *deeply and fully*, the Light of Christ. I can trust that the conscience given to both myself and others will, in the Lord's time, teach both myself and others what is needed—it will do what needs to be done.

> For as the rain cometh down, and the snow from heaven, and returneth not thither, but watereth the earth, and maketh it bring forth and bud, that it may give seed to the sower, and bread to the eater. So shall my word be that goeth forth out of my mouth: it shall not return

---

[82] *Gandhi*, directed by Richard Attenborough, 1982.
[83] Moroni 7:16.
[84] 2 Nephi 32:3.

unto me void, but it shall accomplish that which I please, and it shall prosper in the thing whereto I sent it.[85]

God doesn't choose to do things to fail.

The Light of Christ will work, though likely not always in the time frame we would like. It will "accomplish that which [He] please[s]."

In other words, at some point, those smiting us will "get it." They will understand in perfect humility or perhaps perfect shame what they have done. The Light of Christ is given the role of teacher, not us.

Again, it is not my job to point out my neighbor's sins and lecture them into repenting. (That said, as a parent, I *do* have the responsibility to teach my children, to help them recognize and follow their conscience and bring them up in light and truth.)

Next, please consider the following quote by C.S. Lewis:

> *Christianity asserts that every individual human being is going to live for ever . . . Now there are a good many things which would not be worth bothering about if I were going to live only seventy years, but which I had better bother about very seriously if I am going to live for ever. Perhaps my bad temper or my jealousy are gradually getting worse—so gradually that the increase in seventy years will not be very noticeable. But it might be absolute hell in a million years: in fact, if Christianity is true, Hell is the precisely correct technical term for what it would be.[86]*

Take a moment to let the first sentence of the above quote sink in. You. And. I. Are. Going. To. Live. Forever.

What are the true implications of living forever?

Realize that the person who is "smiting" you is going to live forever, too. They are going to live forever, because Christ loved them enough to die for them, just as He did for you.

Having this perspective is so important.

---

85 Isaiah 55:10-11.

86 Lewis, *Mere Christianity*, 74, emphasis added.

When someone is smiting us, know that this person will still be around in a year, a century, and a trillion years from now—and that Christ died for them too.

Does knowing this affect things?

If you combine this knowledge that they will live forever with the knowledge that the Light of Christ inside them can be trusted, does that change things in your mind? Will the knowledge that Christ literally suffered and died for them help you be willing to suffer a bit for them as well?

Think about it.

Then, consider this quote from C.S. Lewis:

> It is a serious thing to live in a society of possible gods and goddesses, to remember that the dullest and most uninteresting person you can talk to may one day be a creature which . . . you would be strongly tempted to worship, or else a horror and a corruption such as you now meet, if at all, only in a nightmare. *All day long we are, in some degree, helping each other to one or other of these destinations.* It is in the light of these overwhelming possibilities, it is with the awe and the circumspection proper to them, that we should conduct all our dealings with one another, all friendships, all loves, all play, all politics. There are no *ordinary* people. You have never talked to a mere mortal.
>
> *Next to the Blessed Sacrament itself, your neighbor is the holiest object presented to your senses.*[87]

Now, consider how realizing that your neighbor is the holiest object presented to your senses AND that we are all going to live forever AND that we can trust the Light of Christ to teach us and others "all things what [we] should do."[88]

---

[87] Lewis, *The Weight of Glory*, 45-46, emphasis added.
[88] 2 Nephi 32:3.

120

Consider how we are helping each other to either become gods and goddesses or horrors and corruptions met only in a nightmare.

So the next time someone "smites" you, can you turn the other cheek and think the following about the person smiting you?

1) You are my brother or sister for eternity, a child of God with infinite potential. There are mountains of good in you—even if you are acting your worst right now. I am going to try my best to see it.

2) As such, the Light of Christ will eventually teach you the consequences of your actions toward me, and you will eventually perfectly understand what you have done to me. I will trust the Light of Christ to do this.

3) I believe and trust in the good in you, AND I very much value my long-term relationship with you—a relationship that can possibly last more than a trillion years, even eons.

4) So, when you get it (be it in a second or two, a year, ten years, or a million years or more), as a hopefully more perfected being, I hope you will look back on this moment and know that I saw and believed in the good in you—I saw the god in embryo in you and had full confidence that you would get it and so didn't need to do or say anything back—other than perhaps to express love to you. I choose to take the gazillion-year perspective, with you and I hopefully looking back on this simply as adults would look on a toddler having a bad day or throwing a tantrum. I imagine you coming to yourself with the help of the Light of Christ, making it better (repenting), and you and I laughing it off, perhaps a million years from now.

5) I will give you your dignity until then, just as Christ is giving me my dignity by giving me time to repent of my own sins. Christ will teach you when the time is right. I can count on that.

By simply turning the other cheek and refusing to "hit back" or argue further, we give each other our dignity and love the good in each of us. We will all get it—even if it takes a long, long time—we can trust that. Our God knows all about what lies beneath the surface of a soul, and He has made and knows our very deepest selves.

This same God has asked us to turn the other cheek to each other.

This isn't about karma, which is getting what you deserve. It is about Grace, which is giving people what they don't deserve—just like Christ has and is doing for us.

Being the one who gives Grace may be hard, but it helps us be like Christ. And that is the point, for all of us.

Remember, God loved us enough to give us this life to try to learn to be like Christ. He is going to give us opportunities to practice. And though it may seem hard, and we may question why, remember, love really is the answer.

Real Truth Exists

There really is right and wrong. There is such a thing as eternal truth—truth that is independent of what anyone else thinks about it— that is real whether it is believed or not.

Fasting

Remember: when you need extra power from heaven, there is added power in fasting:

> And when they were come to the multitude, there came to him a certain man, kneeling down to him, and saying, Lord, have mercy on my son: for he is lunatic, and sore vexed: for ofttimes he falleth into the fire, and oft into the water. And I brought him to thy disciples, and they could not cure him.
>
> Then Jesus answered and said, O faithless and perverse generation, how long shall I be with you? how long shall I suffer you? bring him hither to me. And Jesus rebuked the devil; and he departed out of him: and the child was cured from that very hour.
>
> Then came the disciples to Jesus apart, and said, Why could not we cast him out?
>
> And Jesus said unto them, Because of your unbelief: for verily I say unto you, If ye have faith as a grain of mustard seed, ye shall say unto this mountain, Remove hence to yonder place; and it shall remove; and nothing

shall be impossible unto you. Howbeit this kind goeth
not out but by prayer and fasting.[89]

I don't know what it is about fasting, but there is something about
it that gives us extra power. I sometimes wonder if God knows we are
really pleading when we fast, not just asking Him with our words, but
with our actions as well.

---

[89] Matthew 17:14–21.

The Little Things Are the Big Things

For want of a nail the shoe was lost;
For want of a shoe the horse was lost;
For want of a horse the battle was lost;
For the failure of battle the kingdom was lost—
All for the want of a horse-shoe nail.[90]

I have the pleasure of knowing a young man who I will call Mark.[91] Mark is a bright, young recent graduate from an Ivy League's top-tier MBA program who is enjoying a successful career with one of the largest tech companies in the world. In preparation to attend graduate school, Mark took the GMAT (the test required by most schools to get into an MBA program) and achieved a score so high it was in the 99th percentile.

Now, before I get more into Mark's story, let's look at what it means to graduate from an Ivy League MBA program. There are many benefits, from the satisfaction that comes from doing something difficult to the prestige of having a top-tier education to the personal satisfaction of

---

90 Proverb of unknown origin
91 Name has been changed to protect anonymity. Also, I discussed this with Mark more than once, and so I am paraphrasing here my recollection of multiple in-person and written conversations into one.

knowing that your increased knowledge can help you positively impact the world. Though this personal satisfaction is not concretely measurable, these psychological benefits are very real and perhaps more important than other perks. However, most Ivy League school grads also make more money than others, and though monetary reward may not be the best yardstick, it is a bit more measurable. So, let's examine it:

According to Bloomberg, the typical Stanford MBA graduate makes about $285,000 per year after being out of school for six to eight years.[92] Compare this with the median American household income, which in 2016 totaled $59,039 annually[93]. Thus, a typical Stanford MBA graduate makes about $225,961 more than a typical American household just six to eight years after graduation. Assuming a typical Stanford graduate works for another thirty years after that, simple math would say that a Stanford grad stands a good chance of making around $6.8 million more than an average American household over the course of their lifetime ($225,961 x 30 years = $6,778,830).

I was curious about what Mark did to get accepted to Stanford, so I did what any curious person might do—I asked him.

"What did you do to get into Stanford?" I inquired, thinking it was possible that his success was because of an expensive GMAT prep course or that he had been privileged enough to attend an expensive private school or something else.

His answer was surprising: "If there was a word I didn't understand, I would have to look it up in the dictionary."

Stunned, I didn't say what I was thinking: *Looking stuff up in the dictionary can get you into Stanford?*

"Tell me more," I begged.

"After that, it became exponential," Mark continued. "Because I understood what people were talking about, I could then make other

---

[92] Nasiripour, Shahien, "Why Stanford MBAs Earn the Most." Bloomberg Business Week (2017).

[93] Semega, Jessica L., "Income and Poverty in the United States: 2016." United States Census Bureau.

mental connections that I would not have made if I hadn't taken the time to look it up."

Mark continued, "If I had a question about anything, I would ask my dad (I assumed he knew everything, and he knows a lot). If he didn't know the answer, or if he wanted to 'teach me how to fish,' he would say, 'Let's look it up.' Then we would go to the dictionary or scriptures or whatever. But once the question was asked, we always looked for the answer. This was something he got from my grandma, who also had a deep love of learning. The mindset of not being content with not knowing is one that still impacts me today."

"Was there anything else you did?" I asked, wondering if I had missed something.

"Well, sometimes I had to look up stuff in the encyclopedia," Mark said.

He continued, "I would attribute this to a love of and commitment to learning, something I got from both my parents. The dictionary is one example of this, but I think the mindset is the most important part."

Mark's mindset, a mindset inspired by his father, of looking words up in the dictionary or encyclopedia, set in motion the insatiable curiosity and passion for learning that made all the difference for Mark. These connections were planted, nurtured, and embedded in neural pathways in Mark's brain by a loving parent, who happened to get that from his own loving parent, Mark's grandma—connections that were built and grew slowly, just like a farmer's seeds, over time. This eventually allowed him to score in the 99th percentile on the GMAT and get into Stanford's MBA program, a program so sought after that it has an acceptance rate just over half that of Harvard.

Later, I went home and did some math:

If you assume Mark was correct—that looking up words in the dictionary and encyclopedia *is what* got him into Stanford and that if he hadn't, he would have had an income closer to that of the median American household, then Mark may have been banking at least $2,190 per hour in future earnings by looking stuff up in the dictionary as an elementary through college student! And this is a conservative estimate![94]

Do any of you have elementary school children making $2,190 per hour?!

Now, let's be clear. No one was cutting Mark a check at the end of each hour, day, week, or even month. The payoff will not likely come until much later. But his choices as a youth led to the possibility of millions of dollars in future earnings. Most people would not believe that looking stuff up in a dictionary or encyclopedia could bring that kind of return. But it might for Mark. Interestingly, much more important to Mark is that attending Stanford will optimize his (1) learning, (2) adventure, and (3) lifetime positive impact. The earning potential was just a side benefit.

Remember that, like gravity, human relations principles are ancient and timeless and are "there" whether we respect them or not.

What was the principle that Mark was aligning with?

---

[94] To reach that figure, we are assuming that he averaged a full thirty minutes a day every single day, both while he was in school and during the summer when not in school for an entire seventeen years, or kindergarten through four years of college [though it is unlikely that as a kindergartner Mark spent a full thirty minutes each day looking up things he didn't understand]. If these estimates are right, easy math would show that Mark spent a total of 3,102.5 hours [17 years x 365 days per year x 30 min per day] looking stuff up. Divide 3,102.5 hours into our conservative estimate of $6.8 million, and we can calculate he could have been making around $2,190 per hour looking stuff up in the dictionary—before he even graduated from college. Please note that these estimates do not take into account inflation or cost of living increases. If inflation and cost of living increases were included, the estimated hourly rate would almost certainly be much higher.

Really think about this

before turning the page

I believe that Mark was aligning with the Law of the Harvest—a principle that literally governs our lives in much the same way that gravity does.

The Law of the Harvest states that we reap what we sow—a farmer will be able to harvest in the fall the exact plants he planted as seeds in the spring—if he nurtures, waters, and weeds the ground surrounding the seeds that he planted.

I once presented to a group that included several farmers, and we were discussing the Law of the Harvest. At one point, I asked them if they thought one could cheat the principle of the Law of the Harvest.

They laughed.

Farmers, more than any other profession, understand this principle as well as any other. They deal almost daily with the principle, and they know that trying to cheat it would be as futile as pretending that gravity doesn't work.

We reap what we sow.

What we put out will come back to us.

What we fail to sow, we will fail to reap.

And, like gravity, we can align with these principles or ignore them to our peril.

Many parents want a silver bullet or the next big thing to make them successful parents. Many look for the "secret" to success, the next fad or program that can help them get where they want to go. They want something big, something powerful, to take them there. However, what many parents need is not what they think. They don't need the next big thing, program, or idea. They just need to discover or learn what principles govern getting to where they would like to go. In almost every case, the Law of the Harvest is one of these principles.

Then, they need to choose to align their little, tiny daily decisions with that principle—decisions so small most think they don't matter.

But these decisions do matter—more than you might think. These little, tiny decisions are exactly like the little, tiny seeds that farmers plant in hopes of a harvest.

In fact, the little, tiny decisions we make each day can literally be the difference between success and failure.

Like the Law of the Harvest, Mark's possible future success was not something he could cram for. His success came, in part, because of *the small choice, the tiny choice, made over and over each day*, to follow his father's advice.

And to take it a step further, the small, tiny choice that Mark's father made to inspire Mark to "look it up" will likely affect generations to come.

Again, parenting is really the ultimate career.

It is the most important work in the world.

Remember how parenting really means more, in the long run, than anything else you ever do?

As a wise friend once told me, "Don't worry about the big stuff. If you worry about the little things, the big things will be taken care of."

And he's right, in so many ways.

Take, for example, the seemingly simple choice to exercise. Most people acknowledge that exercising each day is good for you but may forget just how good it is for you and for whatever reason don't make the choice to get up and do it. The Centers for Disease Control website indicates that exercising for 150 minutes a week (around 22 minutes a day) significantly reduces the risk of cardiovascular disease, type 2 diabetes, and some cancers. The CDC also indicates exercise can help with better sleep, increased energy, and decreased risk of depression.[95] So, if you want to possibly avoid BIG health problems and enjoy a better life, making a little, tiny daily choice to exercise may help.

As another example, many people have had the unfortunate experience of being second place in a relationship with someone who feels they cannot live without their cell phone and who checks it constantly. Perhaps the cell phone addict thinks that the next text message, social media post, or email is more important than the person

---

[95] "Benefits of Physical Activity." Center for Disease Control.

sitting right in front of them—if not true, their actions imply as much. They may not realize that a recent study suggests how something as simple as turning off your cell phone could mean the difference between a failed relationship and one that lasts.

In yet another example, many parents don't realize that the tiny, daily choice of whether to read to their kids or simply hand them an electronic device has huge consequences. It is well known now that daily reading out loud to children has been shown to affect literacy, cognitive development, and social skills and has an actual biological impact on young brains and their ability to learn later in life. In other words, taking the easy way and handing your kids a phone to entertain them might, in the long run, contribute to them being less successful than taking the time to read with them. If you really want to think long-term, realize that reading level is often passed from one generation to the next. So, a consistent daily choice to entertain children with a screen of some sort instead of reading to them could affect literally generations to come. Still, many parents default to letting television, the internet, and video games raise their children—literally. The statistics are staggering: one report indicates children over eight spend an average of over seven hours a day in front of screens.[96]

If you want to be successful in any endeavor, look at the choices that you think don't make a difference. Perhaps you are spending an extra thirty minutes reading news on the internet or watching TV—time that could be used to learn something new, exercise, mend a distressed relationship, or start a side business. Perhaps you are sleeping in a little or staying up too late. Perhaps you are in the habit of arguing when it would be best to bite your tongue. Or you remain quiet when it would be best to stand up and say something. Perhaps your phone apps are getting more attention than the people you care about, or your children are getting more time with your phone apps than with you.

I'm not saying you should never have down time or that every minute needs to be spent doing something "productive." In fact, the

---

[96] "Generation M2." Kaiser Family Foundation.

opposite is more likely true—the choice to slow down and meditate, read good literature, or spend time alone in nature may be the daily choice that helps you get clear on your direction so that your other daily choices move you where you really want to go. What I am saying is to start paying attention to the choices that don't seem like they matter.

Many people don't think that regularly looking up words you don't understand in the dictionary could mean millions of dollars, or that consistently putting down the cell phone could save a marriage, or that taking a brisk run each day could make the difference between seeing your great-grandchildren or having them see your gravestone—but these little daily choices can—and much of the time do—make all the difference.

Your little, tiny daily decisions truly are your big decisions. They determine what you will harvest, because whether you believe it or not, the principle of the Law of the Harvest is working in your life and in the lives of your children.

It doesn't matter whether you believe in gravity or the Law of the Harvest.

It's there and it works. Mark aligned with it. Some ignore it, to their peril.

When you align with the Law of the Harvest, you look to the future with excitement. When you ignore the Law of the Harvest, it is much more probable that you will look to the future with worry and fear.

Your little decisions ARE your big decisions, because your little decisions are the seeds you are planting each day, and like it or not—the principle of the Law of the Harvest has and will always be working.

Remember, you can choose to do whatever you want, but you do not control the consequence. Principles do.

Principles

Are.

Determining.

The.

Consequences.

Of.
Your.
Choices.
Right.
Now.
This.
Moment.

Align or ignore.

Starting the Day Out Right

*It comes the very moment you wake up each morning. All your
wishes and hopes for the day rush at you like wild animals. And
the first job each morning consists simply in shoving them all back;
in listening to that other voice, taking that other point of view,
letting that other larger, stronger, quieter life come flowing in. And
so on, all day. Standing back from all your natural fussings and
frettings; coming in out of the wind.*[97]

I have found that waking up early is one of the great pleasures of
life. I enjoy getting up early so that I can pray and then listen. I often
find answers while reading the scriptures and then record my
impressions so that I can remember them.

There is something wonderful and deeply calming about praying in
silence and reading scriptures and meditating in the morning. There is
something deeply calming when, in quiet and alone with God, you ask
Him how you can be an instrument in His hands.

And then listen.

I believe that if we will take time to pray and meditate and listen to
and then record and act on God's promptings in the morning, we will
be in a much better position to have success during the day.

---

[97] Lewis, *Mere Christianity*, 198.

Stephen Covey talks about how many people climb the ladder to success fast and furiously their whole lives, only to find that the ladder is "leaning against the wrong wall."[98]

Spending time listening to our promptings, praying quietly and in secret, and then recording and acting on our promptings is a huge step toward making sure that our ladder is leaning on the right wall.

Direction first, then speed.

Is your ladder leaning on the right wall? Make sure of that first by staying close to God and praying to Him. And the mornings seem like a great time to do that.

---

[98] Covey, *The Seven Habits*, 98.

Truth Mixed with Lies

Be aware: It is almost certain you will experience truth mixed with lies. It will be up to you, with the help of God and your conscience, to discern which part is true and which part is a lie.

Much advertising is a lie wrapped in truth, or a truth with a sprinkling of lies. Some religion is truth mixed with a lie or a lie(s) mixed with truth.

Remember, we are in enemy territory—so this is to be expected. Why does this happen? Mixing truth with lies strengthens the lies, and the enemy knows this. Christ, and simply Christ alone, is the Most Important Thing.

In C.S. Lewis's book *The Screwtape Letters*, a master devil trying to train an apprentice devil about how best to tempt men to do evil says this:

> What we want, if men become Christians at all, is to keep
> them in the state of mind I call 'Christianity And'. You
> know—Christianity and the Crisis, Christianity and the
> New Psychology, Christianity and the New Order . . . If
> they must be Christians let them at least be Christians
> with a difference. Substitute for the faith itself some
> Fashion with a Christian colouring.[99]

---

[99] Lewis, C.S., *The Screwtape Letters*, (Geoffrey Bles, 1942), 135.

The point is to mix the truth of Jesus Christ with something that not only separates Christians but is also at least partially not true.

Now, consider this quote about Lewis's famous character, Lucy, from the Chronicles of Narnia (*The Last Battle*, to be exact):

> Then she understood the devilish cunning of the enemies' plan. By mixing a little truth with it they had made their lie far stronger.[100]

I once attended a dinner where a slideshow was presented by a person wanting to sell a health cure. He was using a PowerPoint presentation and was flipping through the slides in front of a somewhat large and unsuspecting audience. It was alarming and sad to see a slide of truth followed by a slide that definitely had a lie, then followed by more slides that had truth. Sadly, I think many people assumed that all the slides were basically true. It really took someone with knowledge who was paying close attention to see that some of the slides were not true.

An approach of the devil is to mix the truth that God exists with lies about God's nature (*how* God actually *is*).

Consider this quote from C.S. Lewis – where he shows how the truth of God is mixed with falsehoods:

> An "impersonal God" —well and good. A subjective God of beauty, truth and goodness, inside our own heads — better still. A formless life-force surging through us, a vast power which we can tap —best of all. But God Himself, alive, pulling at the other end of the cord, perhaps approaching at an infinite speed, the hunter, king, husband —that is quite another matter.[101]

What is the real truth?

What is real, whether we believe it or not?

Are we willing to look for truth, even if we don't like what we find?

---

[100] Lewis, C.S., *The Last Battle*, (The Bodley Head., 1956), 102.
[101] Lewis, *Miracles*, 94.

Or will we only look for truth if it agrees with what we want to believe?

Be careful of lies mixed with truth—especially lies mixed with the strongest truth of all—Jesus Christ. Satan uses this same tactic. He will wrap lies in lots of truth. I think he may do it for at least two reasons:

1) The truth camouflages the lie for a while—at least in the beginning.
2) When the lie is finally exposed at the end, many people think the truth that was mixed in with the lie—was also a lie.

For example, many people have believed in both Christ and false leaders. When the false leader is exposed, many leave the movement/religion disillusioned and then decide that Christ is a lie as well. In *The Last Battle*, the formerly loyal Dwarfs sadly lost faith in the real Aslan (a representation of Christ) precisely because they did not want to be deceived again, as they had fallen for the false prophet (the Ape) and his false Aslan. Thus, when the real Aslan showed up, they would not believe.[102]

So, Satan can use the lie to deceive both at the beginning and at the end. His ultimate aim is to get people to lose faith in Christ. He is more than willing to throw a few false leaders under the bus if it means that people will lose faith in Christ in the end.

Don't "throw the baby [Christ] out with the bath water [false beliefs, leaders, or other lies mixed in]."

Christ is real, even if the narrative or the people spinning the narrative around Christ mix in lies.

As C.S. Lewis said:

> . . . never, never pin your whole faith on any human being: not if he is the best and wisest in the whole world. There are lots of nice things you can do with sand: but do not try building a house on it.[103]

---

[102] Lewis, *The Last Battle*.

[103] Lewis, *Mere Christianity*, 191.

You will see deception surrounding Christ. You will see false prophets and leaders. You will likely even see false Christs. Discern and remember that the enemy wants people to "fall" for the false leaders/prophets/Christs so that, just like the Dwarfs in *The Last Battle*, eventually they will stop believing in the Real Thing.

Christ Himself said:

> Beware of false prophets, which come to you in sheep's clothing, but inwardly they are ravening wolves. Ye shall know them by their fruits. Do men gather grapes of thorns, or figs of thistles? Even so every good tree bringeth forth good fruit; but a corrupt tree bringeth forth evil fruit. A good tree cannot bring forth evil fruit, neither can a corrupt tree bring forth good fruit. Every tree that bringeth not forth good fruit is hewn down, and cast into the fire.[104]

Then later, regarding His second coming, Jesus said:

> Then if any man shall say unto you, Lo, here is Christ, or there; believe it not. For there shall arise false Christs, and false prophets, and shall shew great signs and wonders; insomuch that, if it were possible, they shall deceive the very elect. Behold, I have told you before. Wherefore if they shall say unto you, Behold, he is in the desert; go not forth: behold, he is in the secret chambers; believe it not. For as the lightning cometh out of the east, and shineth even unto the west; so shall also the coming of the Son of man be.[105]

Remember the words above.

Always believe in Christ.

Always.

---

[104] Matthew 7:15–19.
[105] Matthew 24:23–27.

Christ is real. Christ is true—even if the people talking about Him are not.

Fear and Greed

Compare with me for a minute the following two quotes. The first is from C.S. Lewis:

> Hell is something like the bureaucracy of a police state . . . an official society *held together entirely by fear and greed* . . . "Dog eat dog" is the principle of the whole organisation. Everyone wishes everyone else's discrediting, demotion, and ruin; everyone is an expert in the confidential report, the pretended alliance, the stab in the back. Over all this their good manners, their expressions of grave respect, their "tributes" to one another's invaluable services form a thin crust. Every now and then it gets punctured, and the scalding lava of their hatred spurts out.[106]

Now, consider this quote from Investopedia:

> The *fear and greed* index was developed by CNNMoney to measure on a daily, weekly, monthly and yearly basis two of the primary emotions that influence how much investors are willing to pay for stocks.[107]

---

[106] Lewis, *The Screwtape Letters*, Preface, emphasis added.
[107] Liberto, "Fear and Greed Index." Investopedia.

Do you see the similarity?

Hell, by C.S. Lewis's definition, is held together by *fear and greed*.

Investing, by CNNMoney's definition, is primarily influenced by *fear and greed*.

Fear and greed: the emotions that run hell AND the emotions that, according to Investopedia, run investing.

Remember this quote from C.S. Lewis:

> Enemy-occupied territory—that is what this world is. Christianity is the story of how the rightful king has landed, you might say landed in disguise, and is calling us all to take part in a great campaign of sabotage.[108]

Again, it is important to remember that the enemy is NOT other people.

The enemy is the devil, and division itself—not our fellow human beings. We sabotage the system by believing in the truth—which is that all people are children of God—and by trying, like God, to see the mountains of good in them.

That said, is it possible that a good portion of the financial center of the modern world is really influenced by fear and greed, which has made it almost a shadow of Hell—not the real Hell, but a poor replication of it, a shadow of it in "*enemy-occupied territory*"?

Again, every person on earth is a child of God, including all people in the financial system. All are God's children, whom He loves very much. Sadly, it is likely many feel empty and exhausted by the emotions of fear and greed, even if outwardly they appear wealthy, contented, and happy.

Do we really want to climb to the top rung in the enemy's territory?

Remember—the world is upside down.

1) Investing is, at the moment, one of the most proven ways to get and stay wealthy, and thus improve your social status in this world.

---

[108] Lewis, *Mere Christianity*, 46.

2) If CNNMoney is correct, investing is driven primarily by the hellish emotions of fear (of loss) and greed (the desire to make more).

What's "up" in this world (investing, getting rich) puts you at real risk of going "down" in Christ's Real World, if you let the emotions of fear and greed rule your heart.

Christ, the King of the Real World, wants us to be completely free of fear and greed. His world, the Real World, is free of it.

To sabotage the enemy-territory emotions of fear and greed, we need to follow the advice of the Rightful King, the Savior Himself, and do exactly opposite of what the world (enemy-occupied territory) teaches us.

Instead of aiming to get rich, consider what the King taught a rich man in His time:

> Then Jesus beholding him loved him, and said unto him, One thing thou lackest: go thy way, sell whatsoever thou hast, and give to the poor, and thou shalt have treasure in heaven: and come, take up the cross, and follow me.[109]

I think it is interesting that the first thing Jesus did after he "beheld," or saw, him was to love him. Continuing:

> And he was sad at that saying, and went away grieved: for he had great possessions. And Jesus looked round about, and saith unto his disciples, How hardly shall they that have riches enter into the kingdom of God! And the disciples were astonished at his words. But Jesus answereth again, and saith unto them, Children, how hard is it for them that trust in riches to enter into the kingdom of God! It is easier for a camel to go through the eye of a needle, than for a rich man to enter into the kingdom of God.[110]

---

[109] Mark 10:21.
[110] Mark 10:22-25.

In other words, we need to kill the part of us that wants to be greedy. Not just try not to be greedy. Not injure the greed. Kill the greed that lives in us entirely, by following the advice of Christ Himself and trading our earthly treasure for treasure in the Real World.

Regarding fear, Jesus said this:

> Peace I leave with you, my peace I give unto you: not as the world giveth, give I unto you. Let not your heart be troubled, neither let it be afraid.[111]

Remember, God is NOT asking us to sabotage any person or thing in the world. He made all people, the world, and all that is in it. He is asking us to take on and sabotage the hellish and controlling emotions of fear and greed. He knows that if money becomes our primary aim, it will destroy us eventually, that we will *fear* losing it, and that we could also *greed*ily want more—He wants to spare us from the hell that comes from fear and greed. We need to be brave enough to be willing to give up our riches. Unfortunately, the rich man's fear of losing his possessions caused him to grieve and be sad.

Anything, if put before Christ, will end up keeping us in Hell. Christ tells us to follow Him because He is literally the only way out of this enemy territory. He is the only way out of Hell. If we put people or money or status, or even seemingly benign things like our spouse or family, in front of Him, things will deteriorate. People and our family and our spouses are so important, but they must come second to Christ. And, crucially, when we put Christ first, our family, our spouse, and other areas of concern will fall into place. He created them. And He knows how important they are. He created us and so knows what will make us happy.

Anything, if put before Christ, will keep us out of the Real World and on the wrong side of the door.

Riches—the whole concept of riches—is really just the concept of comparison, which is really just pride, and it is sewn into the enemy's

---

[111] John 14:27.

propaganda. The real poison is that riches, if put before Christ, inspire pride.

In *The Screwtape Letters*, a master devil tells an apprentice devil how prosperity can help get people to feel more at home in enemy-occupied territory:

> Prosperity knits a man to the World. He feels that he is 'finding his place in it', while really it is finding its place in him.[112]

How do we sabotage the enemy's tools of fear and greed? Again, no matter the question, Love is the answer.

---

[112] Lewis, *The Screwtape Letters*, 155.

Find Your Voice, Then Inspire

Others to Do the Same

God has given you a combination of gifts that only you have.
Just you.

Find out what those gifts are and unleash them.

If you do, your influence and your ability to love and serve others
will be massive.

Then, when you have found what you need to do, help others do
the same.

Just Do It

Jesus said:

> Not every one that saith unto me, Lord, Lord, shall enter into the kingdom of heaven; but he that *doeth* the will of my Father which is in heaven. Many will say to me in that day, Lord, Lord, have we not prophesied in thy name? and in thy name have cast out devils? and in thy name done many wonderful works? And then will I profess unto them, I never knew you: depart from me, ye that work iniquity.[113]

Notice that simply saying, "Lord, Lord," is not enough. You have to actually *do* the will of the Father.

Jesus also said: "If any man will *do* his will, he shall know of the doctrine, whether it be of God, or whether I speak of myself."[114]

He didn't say, if you want to know, just really think about it, or talk about it, or even just pray about it.

He said you have to *do* it.

That means actually try as best you can to do what Jesus commanded. You will know what Jesus actually commanded if you

---

[113] Matthew 7:21–23, emphasis added.
[114] John 7:17, emphasis added.

study and read Matthew 5–7, 10, 13, 18, and 23–25. Try your best to love your enemies, bless them that curse you, and cast the mote out of your own eye first. Do your best to control and repent of anger/lust and of judging others. Do your best to become a peacemaker.

This is hard, hard work.

But if you do it, Jesus promises that you will know whether it is of God or whether He was just speaking of Himself.

Take action and just do it.

The Sacred Now

> The next hour, the next moment, is as much beyond our grasp and as much in God's care, as that a hundred years away. Care for the next minute is just as foolish as care for the morrow, or for a day in the next thousand years—in neither can we do anything, in both God is doing everything.[115]

The devil wants us focusing on the hurts or pleasures of the past, and/or he wants us to neglect the present by constantly focusing on the future. "I will do what I should when _____ happens." This kind of thinking results in lost potential, procrastination, and wasted time and lives.

This is because the devil knows what can happen if people focus their best efforts in the now. The sacred now is where the Savior has asked us to live. It is sacred because it is the only moment in which we can use our power to choose. You cannot use your power of choice to change the past. The future is not here yet. The now is where Christ wants us to live. He doesn't even want us to think about tomorrow.

Christ taught this principle when he said, "Take therefore no thought for the morrow: for the morrow shall take thought for the things of itself."[116]

---

[115] MacDonald, George, *Unspoken Sermons I, II, and III*, (approx. 1867-1869), 80.
[116] Matthew 6:34.

The past cannot be changed. The future is not here. Consider this from *The Screwtape Letters*:

> The Future is, of all things, the thing *least like* eternity. It is the most completely temporal part of time —for the Past is frozen and no longer flows, and the Present is all lit up with eternal rays.[117]

Focus on what you can do today. Then take a step, even if it is small. Then keep taking steps forward every day until you get where you need to go.

It may not feel good to read this. That is okay. If you want to serve God and live up to your potential, roll up your sleeves and get to work. Much of the best work is done when people don't feel like it.

Lead your feelings, and work. Eventually your feelings will follow your actions.

Don't confuse living in the now with the false notion that we should "eat, drink, and be merry, for tomorrow we die."

We need to realize that we are going to live forever. That said, we have only now in which to exercise our ability to choose. Just this moment. Use it well.

---

[117] Lewis, *The Screwtape Letters*, 76, emphasis added.

Satan's Counterfeits

Satan likes to counterfeit the Real Thing by mixing good in with bad.

Here are two examples:

Lust is a substitute for real Christlike love and joy. Excitement is a good thing but is not the Real Thing itself. The devil uses part of the real thing—the excitement of lust—and combines it with a lack of real love to confuse it with genuine love. Real Christlike love and joy has both excitement and Real Love.

Communism is a substitute for living a consecrated life of sharing with others. The devil mixes our noble desires of wanting to give and take care of others but does it with the false principle of force.

The counterfeit can be detected in the lack of free will— communism *forces* people to give; while living a consecrated life is giving what you have to others freely—with *free will*—without coercion or force.

Humility

The principle of humility is so important.

Be humble. For much of my life, I have been way too proud. Don't make the mistake that I have made.

Consider this quote from Proverbs:

> My son, despise not the chastening of the Lord; neither be weary of his correction: For whom the Lord loveth he correcteth; even as a father the son in whom he delighteth.[118]

The Lord corrects those He loves, but we have to be humble enough to not "despise" it or "be weary" of it.

The Sermon on the Mount offers lots of godly guidance and correction. There is no one who is exempt from the need to be corrected by and align with principles given in it.

Now, consider this quote from C.S. Lewis:

> As to 'caring for' the Sermon on the Mount, if 'caring for' here means 'liking' or enjoying, I suppose no one 'cares for' it. Who can *like* being knocked flat on his face by a sledgehammer?

---

[118] Proverbs 3:11-12.

I can hardly imagine a more deadly spiritual condition than that of the man who can read that passage with tranquil pleasure.[119]

It takes bravery and humility to be able to withstand the "sledgehammer" of correction.

Be brave.

Be humble.

C.S. Lewis stated:

> If anyone would like to acquire humility, I can, I think, tell him the first step. The first step is to realise that one is proud. And a biggish step, too. At least, nothing whatever can be done before it. If you think you are not conceited, it means you are very conceited indeed.[120]

Humility is power.

Pride is weakness.

Treating all people you meet like children of God helps them feel loved and will increase your ability to influence them.

Many people make the mistake of treating some people as "important" and others as "not important."

Huge mistake.

In the next life, the Real Life, I am convinced that this distinction doesn't exist.

Pride is the opposite of humility. Consider the following quote about pride:

> Pride gets no pleasure out of having something, only out of having more of it than the next man.[121]

Honestly ask yourself:

Am I working each day so that I can get more riches so that I can *compare* more favorably to others? Do I work so that I can have a better

---

[119] Lewis, *God in the Dock*, 181, emphasis added.

[120] Lewis, *Mere Christianity*, 128.

[121] Lewis, *Mere Christianity*, 122.

title at work, a bigger home, or a nicer car in order to compare favorably to others?

How often do I compare myself to others?

How often do I compete with others?

Am I trying to move up on the social ladder, which is really just a tool of the enemy to get people to *compare* and thus get sucked up in pride?

Or is the reason I really want riches so that I can give them away to refugees, the homeless, and others?

Do I seek riches so that I can "sell whatsoever [I have] and give to the poor,"[122] as Jesus asked the rich man?

Be honest.

If you find that you are not willing to sell everything and give to the poor and that your real reasons for wealth are not in alignment with Christ, consider how to change.

Pray for help.

Christ will help you.

> In God you come up against something which is in every respect immeasurably superior to yourself. Unless you know God as that —and, therefore, know yourself as nothing in comparison —you do not know God at all. As long as you are proud you cannot know God. A proud man is always looking down on things and people: and, of course, as long as you are looking down, you cannot see something that is above you.
>
> *. . . Whenever we find that our religious life is making us feel that we are good —above all, that we are better than someone else —I think we may be sure that we are being acted on, not by God, but by the devil.*[123]

---

122 Mark 10:21.

123 Lewis, *Mere Christianity*, 124-125, emphasis added.

Pride is the root of all sin because when we sin we are basically saying that we know better than God and don't need Him.

Let us pray with all our might that we can stay humble and out of this death trap.

The Best Way to Teach

My brother Leland is a smart guy.

He graduated from Harvard with a master's degree in education. He is passionate about education, and so am I. It seems like nearly every time I talk with Leland, we talk about education, sometimes at length. We love talking about it. One day as we were talking about it, the question came up, "What would be the best way to educate someone if you had unlimited money and resources? What would be the very best way to do it?"

After some discussion, this idea came up: What if you could just follow around the person you wanted to be like? Perhaps you could then learn faster, and better, than you could under the current system.

I know that "following (someone) around" doesn't sound like a very complicated or perhaps even an educated idea, but let me explain:

Let's say that you wanted to be a hedge fund manager. As I write this, hedge fund managers are some of the highest-paid people on the planet today. Top hedge fund managers make hundreds of millions of dollars a year, with some even making north of one billion dollars annually.

Currently, for you to even become employed as a base-level employee at a top-notch hedge fund, you would likely need first to get an undergraduate degree from an accredited first-tier university, probably in finance or in a finance-related field. Then, to help you on your way, you would likely want to get an MBA from an Ivy League business school, requiring a very competitive GPA as an undergraduate, as well as a great score on the GMAT test. You may even want to get a PhD in something that gives you quantitative analysis experience, as well as a designation or two such as a Chartered Financial Analyst or Chartered Alternative Investment Analyst. In addition, many firms may require more, such as demonstrated expertise in public relations or some sort of networking ability. You would also likely need to develop a tolerance for and knowledge of bonus and commission structures. Then, you may need fifteen to twenty years of investment experience.

So, to become a hedge fund manager, not only could it likely take around a decade of higher education/designation experience and hundreds of thousands of dollars in tuition at a school that is very difficult to even get into, but after all that, it could take decades of putting in your time working as an analyst or a researcher and/or other positions before you could become an actual hedge fund manager.

But what if it were possible to take a better route?

What if, instead of doing what most people do, you were instead able to just "follow around" one of the top analysts, then learn exactly what senior management needs to see from a top analyst. After that, you could then follow around a top research associate as you learned to trade. Finally, you could follow around one of the top hedge fund managers in the entire world. What if you were able to sit in on every meeting she attends and listen in to every phone call she makes? And because of this, you were able to meet personally the people that she meets with, make the connections she makes, and observe firsthand what criteria she uses to decide whether or not to invest in a particular business? What if you could learn from someone making nine or ten figures a year her criteria for whether to buy or sell a position in a particular business? What if you were able to listen to her phone conversations even after she leaves the office? What if you could watch how she leads a board meeting? What if you could see how she handles potential clients wanting money from her? See her at each meeting? See how or even whether she responds to each email? Hear her private conversations with each staff member? What if you were able to see who and why and how she hired and fired employees or other senior management, and then actually sit in on each interview? What if you could literally just follow this ultra-successful person around?

What kind of an education would you be getting? Would you learn faster? Do you think it is possible that you could become a great hedge fund manager in a much shorter time, rather than a few decades?

Wouldn't "following around" a hedge fund manager who is actually making hundreds of millions of dollars a year and seeing what she did in real life beat attending endless dry lectures by college professors who are likely making a fraction of what she is? (As I write this, the average college professor makes less than $100k a year.)

Wouldn't "following around" a real-life example of what you want to be, be better than listening to someone who may not be doing it in real life?

Don't you think you could learn more in a few months or years by following around one of the best hedge fund managers in the world than you could trying to work your way up the ladder, learning from college professors and other, less-experienced employees, spending over twenty to thirty years in the current system?

I am convinced that "following around" the person you want to be like is probably the best way to become what you want to be. It is the best way to educate people. Some leaders in the business and education world seem to be catching on to this. They use such terms as "shadow leadership," "tutorial approach," "apprenticeship approach," and "mentoring." But really, it is just following around the person you want to be like.

After this conversation with my brother, I was sitting in my car at a stop light, when a thought came to me. It hit me harder than a semi truck barreling through the intersection. Here it is:

The best way to educate people has been around forever.

It's called parenting.

We get to have little people, who learn faster than adults and who desperately want to be like us, follow us around for eighteen years—sometimes more.

These little people are our own children.

And whether we realize it or not, we are employing the most powerful way to teach during the time they are most teachable just by being a parent and letting them follow us around.

This is an awesome opportunity and scary at the same time.

It's awesome because if we are doing awesome, we can help our children be awesome.

It's scary because we are always teaching. Even when we aren't consciously thinking about it. We don't get to walk out of the classroom. We are always in the classroom, leading what is being taught.

Years ago, I was working as a real estate agent for a home builder in a very challenging market. There were so few buyers that it was decided we would knock on doors to try to find some renters to buy homes. For liability reasons, they sent us out in groups of two. One day, something happened that left an impression on me: After we knocked on one particular door, a child came to the door and told us something like this: "My mom told me to tell you that she can't come to the door because she is in the bathroom." Then, from behind the door, you could hear the mom (who was obviously not in the bathroom) saying to the child, "Okay, dear, shut the door now."

Many would think that this is just a funny story. And in some ways, it is exactly that. At the time, we just kind of laughed and went on to the next door.

However, as I thought about it later, something occurred to me. Here was a mom who obviously, for whatever reason, didn't want to talk to us at the door. I don't blame her—it's a fact that most people don't want to talk to salespeople at their door.

But the way she handled it deserves discussion.

I don't think that mother woke up that morning and thought, "Today I am going to use the best teaching method in the entire world to teach my child to lie."

I really don't think she thought that.

But that is exactly what she did.

She taught her child that if she is in an uncomfortable situation, it is okay to lie. And she did it using the best way to teach people—her example.

Scary.

Spend some time to think about what you are doing as a parent. Then ask yourself:

What am I teaching my children using the best way I can possibly teach someone?

And then remember:

There are three things that are important when teaching others:

1) example

2) example

3) example

I learned this later than I should have.

I am trying to make up for it. And to tell the truth, I don't think I have it even close to down yet.

Still, the little choices we make each day really are the big choices, *especially* when teaching our children.

Sustainable Growth

There is no royal road to anything, one thing at a time, all things in succession. That which grows fast, withers as rapidly. That which grows slowly, endures.[124]

Keep this in mind when you are building—building relationships, getting your education, raising your children, building your spiritual strength and resilience.

Stay away from the quick fixes. As a general rule, they don't work and, in the long run, lead to more frustration and problems.

Don't try to fix your marriage, your family, your career, with the next quick fix. Don't try to get rich quickly. Instead, focus on the slow game. The slow game is the principle of the Law of the Harvest, which says we reap what we have sown. Implicit in this is the fact that crops grow slowly. They don't pop up overnight. You have to till the earth to make sure it is amenable to seeds: you might nourish the soil with fertilizer, manure, or other nutrients. Then you have to plant the seed, water it. Throughout the growing period, you need to make sure it has adequate water and make sure the plants are not choked by weeds. And if you do this long enough, months later you can have a harvest.

---

124 Holland, Josiah Gilbert. *A Dictionary of Quotations in Prose*, 401.

Roll up your sleeves. Work on yourself first. Work on being the kind of spouse you would want to be married to. Fertilize your mind: consider taking classes together, learning together. Take the time to learn the principles of happy marriages and child-raising from people who actually have good marriages and families. Learn how to water the positive things your spouse and children do, rather than giving precious attention to watering the negative weeds. There should be several times more positive interactions than negative.

Practice. Weed the negative out of yourself so that its roots can't strangle the good seeds in your relationships. Water the positive in other people by giving them attention for the positive things they do.

Take the time to figure out what gifts God has given you. Take the time to study out in your mind what the best course of action is, and then get a good education based on that.

Go slow.

Be patient.

Life is often a step or two forward and then a step back. Keep moving forward. Even if it is not fast or you get set back, keep moving and things will work out.

Consider this quote attributed to Calvin Coolidge:

> Nothing in this world can take the place of persistence. Talent will not; nothing is more common than unsuccessful men with talent. Genius will not; unrewarded genius is almost a proverb. Education will not; the world is full of educated derelicts. Persistence and determination alone are omnipotent.[125]

Remember that persistence beats talent, genius, and education. Persistence and determination are more powerful by far.

Direction is more important than speed. Once you get the direction down and align with real principles, the fruits will start to come—often more quickly than you anticipated, if you are persistent and determined.

---

[125] Kerpen, Dave. "17 Quotes to Inspire Persistence." Inc.com

Time

Time is the most valuable asset you have access to.

It is not yours. It is God's gift to you.

Use it to serve God—you do that by serving others.

If—

When I was young, my dad had us memorize scriptures and sometimes poems. My dad is a beacon of consistency and of trying hard even when things are particularly painful. I remember my dad encouraged me to memorize this poem, entitled *If—*, by Rudyard Kipling:

> If you can keep your head when all about you
> Are losing theirs and blaming it on you,
> If you can trust yourself when all men doubt you,
> But make allowance for their doubting too;
> If you can wait and not be tired by waiting,
> Or being lied about, don't deal in lies,
> Or being hated, don't give way to hating,
> And yet don't look too good, nor talk too wise:
> If you can dream—and not make dreams your master;
> If you can think—and not make thoughts your aim;
> If you can meet with Triumph and Disaster
> And treat those two impostors just the same;
> If you can bear to hear the truth you've spoken
> Twisted by knaves to make a trap for fools,
> Or watch the things you gave your life to, broken,
> And stoop and build 'em up with worn-out tools:

If you can make one heap of all your winnings
And risk it on one turn of pitch-and-toss,
And lose, and start again at your beginnings
And never breathe a word about your loss;
If you can force your heart and nerve and sinew
To serve your turn long after they are gone,
And so hold on when there is nothing in you
Except the Will which says to them: 'Hold on!'
If you can talk with crowds and keep your virtue,
Or walk with Kings—nor lose the common touch,
If neither foes nor loving friends can hurt you,
If all men count with you, but none too much;
If you can fill the unforgiving minute
With sixty seconds' worth of distance run,
Yours is the Earth and everything that's in it,
And—which is more—you'll be a Man, my son![126]

My dad lived this poem in many ways. After contracting Stage 4 lung cancer, I never heard him complain. In fact, as I write this, despite his cancer, he is consistently upbeat and almost never mentions his cancer unless asked. And then, even when asked about his cancer, he almost always downplays it and diverts his attention to the person he is talking to.

My dad did not complain when his wife died and left him a widower at age 34 with seven children. He pressed on. After my mother's death, he married again—to my mother Patty. To her credit, she was willing to take on a widower with seven children and she speaks positively of my mother who passed away, even though she never met her. As an adult, I realize what a monumental task it was for her to be a fill-in mother to seven children that weren't hers. She is a loving and supportive Grandma to my children. I am grateful for all she has done.

---

[126] Kipling, Rudyard, *Rewards and Fairies*, (1910), 200-201.

I am grateful that my dad encouraged me to memorize this poem and for living it in many ways.

The Golden Rule

The principle of the Golden Rule, that we should treat others as we want to be treated, is timeless. Like an ancient tree (and gravity), it has been around for a long, long time.

Its branches—Honesty, Patience, Fairness, Kindness—are timeless and are ingrained in the conscience of people everywhere. In fact, there is evidence of the Golden Rule in virtually every hemisphere, culture, and religion, even though it may be called by a different name.

It's everywhere, just like gravity. And, just like gravity, you can align with or ignore it. Learning this principle in my parents' home decades ago not only has benefited others around me, but has even tremendously assisted me in building my business.

Let me give you an example:

Years ago, I had a problem with my account at the bank. I decided to make a visit to the branch to try and fix the problem. The truth was that I had neglected to make a needed transfer into my account, and I now had a bank account that was in the red and had amassed quite a few overdraft fees. The employee who helped me (let's call him Jeff) was very professional and helpful and spent quite a bit of time trying to get a troubling issue resolved for me, even waiving some of the fees. After all his time and effort, I said, "I would like to get the email address of your boss so that I can tell him how professional and helpful you have been."

Jeff looked at me in surprise. It was clear from the way he reacted that Jeff was used to handling complaints and negative situations, rather than handling people who wanted to compliment him, especially to his boss. Later I wrote an email to Jeff's boss and mentioned that Jeff should be recognized and that he was an asset to the company. I copied Jeff on the email.

A while later, I visited the same branch and was surprised at what happened.

I was standing at the back of a line behind several other people waiting for the next available teller, when a bank employee approached me. It was not Jeff. It was not the bank manager either.

"Mr. Anderson, can I help you with something?" the bank employee asked.

"Yes," I said, a bit taken aback. It was not typical to be approached by a banker while at the back of the line. On top of that, I did not recognize this employee, but it was clear that he recognized me.

The bank employee then escorted me from the back of the line, took me to his desk, and allowed me to handle my banking business before several people that were ahead of me in line. I had been to this branch many times before and had not been treated like this. You would have thought I had ten million dollars in the bank—though we all know that I didn't. Though surprised, I felt like I was one of their very special banking customers.

It didn't stop there. I was treated similarly by many bank employees (most of whom I had never worked with before). On more than one occasion, a bank employee would recognize me, call me by name, and allow me to get my banking done ahead of other customers.

What I discovered, almost by accident, was how the Golden Rule works in real life. I had recognized a bank employee who helped me, and now I was being treated as a VIP whenever I visited that branch. It's important that you know that I wrote the letter with no expectation of a response.

It is easy for people to complain, and rude demands seem evermore commonplace. Our children are growing up in this ever more negative world. When someone takes the time to compliment others, especially to someone who has as much influence over their lives as does their boss, it is like a breath of fresh air.

Now, fast forward several years . . .

"I have people call me all day long about your product, but you are the first person that I let into my office about this, and it's because you were nice to my secretary," said Burt, a high-level director at a sizable organization in New York. "I talk to my secretary more than my family, and some salespeople don't understand that."

Being in sales and in a competitive market, I was flabbergasted to learn I was the first salesperson that he had actually met with to discuss my type of product. Competition was fierce in this market, and he had now confirmed that others had wanted to talk to him about it, but he had not been willing to speak with them.

A few weeks prior, I had made a cold call to speak with him. As is almost always the case when calling high-level executives, I was told by his secretary that he was unavailable. I mentioned to his secretary that I had sent an email to him and wondered if I could resend it but copy it to her as well "to make sure that he gets it." She agreed to this.

We chatted for a bit and I noticed that she was very courteous and professional.

At the end of the call, I said to his secretary, "Thank you, Jane, for helping me. I will mention to Burt that you have been very professional and helpful." She seemed a bit taken off guard, but I could tell that she was pleased.

On the first line of the email that I was resending to her boss, I wrote something like this: "I spoke briefly with Jane. She was very professional and helpful."

I then continued with a short note about how I was resending an email I had sent earlier and that I would appreciate an opportunity to meet.

Again, this email was sent to the high-level director and copied to the secretary, Jane, with the first line being a compliment about her. Do you think that Jane had an incentive to show this to her boss?

I had now differentiated myself to Jane from the hundreds of other emails she likely received each month. I was different in her eyes. I cared enough to help her with something she cared about—her job. I had treated the "menial" gatekeeper with the same courtesy and respect as I did someone with greater status. When I showed her and her boss that she mattered and positively reinforced her behavior, I came away with the appointment I wanted. I had been granted a presentation, while many others were ignored.

That simple, sincere compliment was the key to many successful business ventures with that organization and many others. Being kind to the gatekeeper (someone many salespeople assume has the low job, with no importance or leverage) proved to have more influence than anything else I could have done, and soon I was in the office, face-to-face with a key decision-maker.

I have heard of sales tactics that teach salespeople to act indignant toward the gatekeeper in order to get through and get their way. I disagree with these techniques completely.

Principle: Humility.

In other words:

Everyone is

important.

Everyone.

If I had come into the bank and shown indignation, angrily demanding service, I may have had someone fix the problem in the short run, but in the long run the employees would probably avoid me. Appointments with the right people sometimes take a while to get. Acting indignant in the short run will kill your prospects in the long run. Again, aligning with the Golden Rule, a principle as powerful and far-reaching as gravity, has given me business success and even the ability to train others in business.

The truth is that this principle was learned long ago, as a child. You see, my success in sales was really created by loving parents who, many years ago, taught me about the Golden Rule.

As the saying goes, honey works better than vinegar.

This timeless principle can help you find success in all aspects of life. To treat some people as important and others as less important is a type of snobbery. When you treat the janitor with the same courtesy and respect as you treat a CEO, you demonstrate true inner character. When you treat your husband or wife and children with the same level of respect as your employer or a high-level government figure, even when they may not, at the moment, return that respect, you show real integrity. "Influential" people are not more important than "noninfluential people." Remember that the world is indeed upside down. Those on the bottom of this world are often at the top of God's Real World.

It is important to note that we should not treat others as we want to be treated only so that we can get something in return. The real magic happens when we decide that we are going to treat people as we want to be treated, regardless of how they treat us.

Acknowledgment and Recognition

People like to be acknowledged and recognized.

Billions of dollars are spent each year on recognizing noteworthy performers. Does that number seem high? Think company incentive trips and prizes. Think the Oscars! Praise and recognition go a long way, and they can go a long way when influencing anyone.

Acknowledging and recognizing anyone is effectively a three-step process:

1. Find something that you can honestly and sincerely compliment them on.
2. Give them attention for it—the more public, the better!
3. Repeat at random and unexpected times—though make the *way* you reinforce it different each time.

These simple steps will do wonders for your ability to love and influence people.

Remember, the principle of recognizing others is timeless.

Again, be sincere and honest. Most people are doing a lot of things right but are getting little or no attention for it.

Thus, it shouldn't be hard to sincerely find something positive about someone and give them attention publicly. It is especially good to praise people in front of other people they care about—their spouse, their children, their boss, or valued friends.

If the person you are trying to influence is not exhibiting positive behavior, which occasionally is the case, don't compliment them. The compliment must be sincere and honest. There have been times when I have chosen not to compliment someone, because the behavior didn't warrant it.

Positive reinforcement is not a new concept. In my study of psychology, I was fascinated to find that positive reinforcement was *much more effective long-term than punishment or negative reinforcement.*

When your child or spouse does something right, it is so much more effective to immediately recognize them rather than to wait and give them attention when they do something wrong.

Again, using recognition to help you influence someone is a simple process: 1) find something to sincerely compliment them on, 2) give them attention for it—publicly if possible, and 3) repeat randomly and at unexpected times.

Remember, positive reinforcement works best when you immediately reinforce the desired behavior.

The principle is that everyone matters—everyone. Look for opportunities to catch your spouse, your children, and others doing something right.

Consider sending a thank-you card, email, or text (or something else) to someone after any positive interaction.

What other ways can you positively reinforce behaviors in your spouse, children, and others you come in contact with? If you truly understand the principle, your imagination and creativity may help you come up with many new ways to do this.

The Center

When we put Jesus Christ first, as the center of our attention and focus, the other areas of our life will fall into their proper places. We do this by reading His actual words in the New Testament and then trying to follow them. If we are only reading articles about Him, or listening to what others are preaching about Him, we are missing it. Get into the New Testament and read Matthew 5–7, 10, 13, 18, and 23–25. Read the four gospels and what He said. Feast on His actual words, not just commentaries, articles, or preaching from others. Then do your best to follow Him as He Himself actually says.

Memorize Scriptures

A little scripture memorization, either personally or with family each day, will have a big effect later.

The scriptures can come to your mind when you need them to help you avoid temptation or parent your children or help a stranger. My dad was a great example of this. He had us memorize scriptures our whole life. They have often come to mind when I needed them most.

Talk about them with your children while you memorize them. When memorizing, repetition is key. Choosing a few scriptures to repeat a couple of times each morning is helpful.

Hidden Treasures

There are a lot of hidden treasures that can be found only when you keep the commandments. I could write a list with a dozen examples, but let me give you just one:

Reading scriptures together, even when your kids can't read yet, has hidden treasures you wouldn't expect (most of the treasures that Christ has hidden in this world are just that—hidden).

Of course, reading scriptures gives you the opportunity to inoculate your children against temptations and challenges that are sure to arise. It is said that the best time to work on problems is when things are calm, before they start. Having daily scripture reading helps prevent a myriad of possible problems before they happen, and you can work on it when you are not in the thick of the problem, while things are calm. For example, you can discuss the importance of not using drugs, the importance of staying active in the church, the importance of the law of chastity, how to stay humble, and feasting on the words of Christ years before children are confronted with temptations.

Make it a habit to have regular scripture study when children are young and receptive. Have it in a calm environment. It will give you the opportunity to have the daily spiritual feasts that both you and they need.

But hidden in this is an extra bonus. Daily scripture study also helps them *immensely* in learning to read and substantially increases their vocabulary, both of which give them an awesome foundation in their schooling. It immerses them in words they often don't understand—yet. Some people ask why you would read words they don't understand yet. And my answer is simple—it's because they don't understand them—yet. Exposing them early means their pliable, receptive minds build neural pathways around these words that benefit them not only by learning the words, but by actually making it much easier for them to learn other things. Having scripture reading each morning gets their brains geared up and in "learning mode" early each and every day – making it easier to learn in school and other places later in the day. When I build neural pathways in my child's brain during scripture study at 6:30 am, the brain is already in "build neural pathways mode" at 9:15 am or so when they walk in to school.

Children's brains are improved substantially when they are in a rich language environment. Letting your kids be immersed in words that they don't yet understand and which are complicated really, really helps their brains with advanced capabilities.

Let even your small children hear you say and use a lot of different words. It's easy to do this while reading scriptures. Exposing them to a lot of words will help them immensely in their education.

I believe that keeping the commandments has many little side benefits that no one knows about, like having kids excel in reading and vocabulary comprehension when you're just keeping the commandment of having daily scripture reading.

These kinds of hidden treasures are everywhere when you keep the "little" commandments. And remember, the little things really are the big things.

The Short-Term Hard Way Is

the Long-Term Easy Way

Take the hard way now in dating, in marriage, in education, in parenting, and in virtually everything.

Why?

Because the hard way is really the easy way in the long run.

Let me give you a few examples:

Let's say that your five-year-old daughter decides to take a candy bar from the store. To make matters worse, you are already running late for an important appointment. No one at the store seemed to notice the theft.

You may be tempted to just let the child have the candy bar so that you can get to your pressing appointment. In addition, taking the child back into the store to return the candy bar could likely be embarrassing, and even annoying to many parents, not to mention inconvenient—you have an appointment to get to!

However, this seeming annoyance is actually an enormous opportunity in disguise (many, if not most, annoyances are), even though it may make you late for your appointment.

Teaching your five-year-old daughter to align with the principle of the Golden Rule that involves not stealing will take some time. You will likely need to explain to her why it is important that we pay for things and not steal them. You will need to take the time to walk her back into the store and give the candy bar back to a store clerk. You may then give her a reasonable consequence, like having her do chores to pay for it. It may take extra time and effort to explain how to do these chores. All of this takes effort and time.

And, just like gravity, you will have a choice to either align with the principle of teaching your children about the Golden Rule, or you can choose to ignore it.

Thus, in the short run, addressing the behavior may be harder, and take more time, than ignoring the behavior.

However, if you take the short-term easy route and just decide that your pressing appointment is more important and don't take the time to teach your child, there will almost certainly be a negative long-term consequence: Your child may not learn the important lesson that it is not okay to steal (i.e., like gravity, she may never learn to align with the timeless principle of Honesty--which is a part of the Golden Rule--and thus, just like ignoring gravity, she may, figuratively, fall off a cliff). If this lesson is not learned when they are young, your children may later on get the opportunity to learn the same lesson from the inside of a jail or prison cell. It could also end up damaging her future family if she doesn't learn to be honest, and thus her children and grandchildren will be affected in ways you likely would never think about as you try to make your appointment on time.

If this happens, your being on time to your precious appointment could cost the community in the form of police salaries, jail/prison officer salaries, costs for the prison itself, judges, attorneys, prison food expenses, and more.

Additionally, having a criminal record could cost your own child in the form of lost job opportunities and income, which over his or her lifetime may total in the hundreds of thousands or even millions of dollars. Your child may lose friends and relationships from lack of trust. Your child may ultimately lose their own self-respect. This mentions nothing of your own stress that comes from seeing your child experience this.

Thus, not taking the opportunity to teach the principle right away can have huge costs—it could, quite literally, make

> your child lose,
>> the community lose,
>>> and you lose.

If you don't teach her, she will almost certainly get the exact same lesson later and likely in a much harsher way—because the stakes are much higher.

Does this sound over the top to you?

Some may think I am taking this too far.

Remember Mark and how looking stuff up in the dictionary could result in millions of dollars – the little things really are the big things.

Ask yourself and think and ponder on this question:

Why do grown adults make choices that cause them to go to prison?

The truth is, adults end up in prison because they didn't learn the lessons needed to keep them out of prison when they were younger.

Period.

If they did, they would not be there.

The short-term hard way (being late or even completely missing your appointment) is the long-term easy way (avoiding possible criminal imprisonment, lost job opportunities—possibly to the tune of millions of dollars, along with huge community costs like policing, courts, and attorneys, not to mention saving yourself from the stress and guilt that comes from seeing your child have to endure consequences that you could have helped her avoid).

Here is another example of how the short-term hard way is really the long-term easy way:

Your same daughter asks you for a peanut butter sandwich.

This happens all the time for many parents—your daughter needs to be fed, and most parents could easily make a child a peanut butter sandwich in about a minute or less. However, what would happen if, instead of just making the sandwich for her, you decided to take the short-term harder and slower way and teach her to do it?

You may start off by asking, "How do you think *you* could make a peanut butter sandwich?"

Then listen.

At first she may complain and even tantrum, "Just make me a peanut butter sandwich!" but if you don't give in, and even make it fun, she might likely go along.

Principle: Let your child do as much as they can for themselves. Don't rush in and do it for them to save time, even though you are faster and better at it.

For example, she may say that she needs bread, jam, and peanut butter or that she will need to get a butter knife to spread the peanut butter and jam.

You could then ask her questions to help her do it herself:

"Do you think you could get the bread and jam and peanut butter?"

"Do you know where it is?"

"What else would you need to do?"

Of course, if she needs help, you could help her, but *only* for what she cannot do herself.

For example, if she doesn't know where the peanut butter is, instead of just showing her or getting it for her, you could ask:

"Where do you think it might be?"

If she answers, "In the pantry," you might reply, "Great, why don't you go see if you can find it in the pantry? I bet you can find it."

Your child will almost certainly love learning something new *if* you are patient and loving as you teach them. I tried letting my daughter make a peanut butter sandwich, and it was fun to see how she smiled from ear to ear and was so proud of herself when she "made a sandwich all by myself" for the first time.

Teaching your child for the first time or two may take much longer than if you just did it yourself. For example, if it took you ten minutes to teach her when you could have easily done it in one minute—(10x longer than just doing it for them), you may have lost ten minutes in the short run.

But guess what you have gained in the long run:

1. A more confident child!
2. Hours and hours of saved time—now she can make her own sandwiches anytime she needs it—for decades!

Forever, actually.

That's why it is important to ask:

"Where will this small choice lead in the long run? A million years from now?"

Let your children do *everything* they reasonably can for themselves. Though it takes more time in the short run, in the long run, letting them go slow and even fail at first makes your children confident and resilient—whereas *doing too much for your children cripples them.*

> Principle: Take the long-term view on everything. Why? Because if Christianity is true, you are going to be alive for a long, long time.

I am not saying to let them break the law, principles, or do things that will harm themselves or others.

Let's face it. You are better than your children at lots of things. This makes it easy in the short run to just do things for them.

I know of many wealthy parents who did more than they should have for their children. Their children are now grown and struggle in multiple ways—including emotionally and financially.

I know of many parents with meager means who now have very successful children.

Granted, being wealthy doesn't mean that your children will automatically struggle, but it does indicate that you need to be careful that you are not doing too much for them.

> Principle: The short-term hard way is the long-term easy way.

Let your children do things around the house. Teach them to work while they are young.

As parents, every day we have choices. We have choices to take the hard way or the easy way. Most of the time, the short-term hard way is really the best way and also the long-term easy way.

I know of parents who neglected to spend time with their family each week and have regular daily scripture study and daily family prayer. Now those families have a child or children who do not believe in Christ or His gospel. It is difficult to make family scriptures and prayer a priority every day. It may be difficult to put a regular weekly family night above work, social, or other pressing concerns. But it is also difficult to see your children not believe, leave the faith, and make choices that will negatively impact them, their loved ones, and their future.

Choose your difficult. Which do you want? The difficulty of having daily scriptures, family prayer, and weekly family nights, or the angst of seeing your children stop believing?

Now, I know of families that have done all of the above and still had children leave the faith. To those families, my words probably sting. Let me lessen that sting now: I believe at some point your efforts will have more power than you can imagine. Your children may not come back until much later, but your efforts are not in vain. I know. There was a time I stopped believing in things I had been taught as a youth, and the words of my mom and dad eventually had more power than you can imagine. Keep faithful. The story is not over.

It may be difficult to cut off a dating relationship in which you are physically attracted to someone but deep down know that they are dishonest and don't have the spiritual or moral foundation to make a successful marriage.

Choose your difficult. Do you want the short-term difficulty of being lonely for a while, missing them, and dealing with the pain of moving on and finding someone better, or do you want the long-term difficulty of a lifelong unhappy relationship that is possibly constantly threatened by cheating and other major problems?

It may be difficult to continue your education when you are trying to find ways to pay for tuition, or you don't feel up to another semester of hard work. But it is also difficult to spend decades being passed over for promotions, or to struggle financially in a business for decades because you didn't put in the effort to learn what you need to be successful.

Choose your difficult. Which do you want? The difficulty of getting a good education or the difficulty of struggling financially later?

It is difficult to work on a marriage that is on the rocks. But it is also difficult to have a divorce and custody battles and watch for decades the ongoing fallout that will touch not only your life but the lives of your children and generations that follow after someone divorces.[127]

Choose your difficult. Which difficult will you choose? The difficulty of working on a marriage, taking classes, learning patience, learning to hash out difficulties, and learning to love an imperfect human being? Or the difficulty of court battles, attorney's fees, damaged children and yes, grandchildren, and seeing the result of your choices playing out again in your own children and grandchildren as fallout that comes with children learning that commitment and covenants are disposable?[128]

Take the short-term hard way—not because I am a sadist and want to see you suffer. On the contrary, I want you to be able to avoid a lot of chronic pain later on.

The short-term hard way is almost always the long-term easy way.

Take the hard way today so your life will work better long-term. And teach your children this and other timeless principles early.

---

[127] When making decisions, it is important to have the Holy Ghost with you. Pray hard that you can know what to do, especially in big decisions like marriage.
[128] Please note, that there may be instances where divorce is appropriate.

When the World Is Upside Down

When the world is upside down:

1) what looks like up is really down, and

2) what looks like down is really up.

Everyone in need of help is Jesus in disguise.

Follow Your Promptings

I have a good friend who inspired me to write down my promptings. A prompting is a thought that comes to your mind—oftentimes at quiet moments, but it could happen anytime or anywhere. It could happen in the middle of the night or even while driving or walking. Most often, for me, it happens when I intentionally take time to be quiet, pray, and listen. So I decided to follow my friend's advice and acquired more than one little book that would help me record some of my promptings.

On December 2, 2019, or close to then, I wrote the following in my promptings journal:

"Take kids to the symphony. Today if possible or very soon."

I wrote it down, even though it seemed a bit odd. However, it seemed like it would be a great family outing to dress up, go out to eat, get on the train, and have a night out downtown at the symphony.

I mentioned this prompting to my wife. She thought it was a bit odd but still agreed to help me find a way to take our children to the symphony. She found an advertisement shortly thereafter that advertised a few different symphonies in our area. We discussed dates and programs. The pricing in some situations was a bit more than either of us wanted to pay, and so we delayed in order to think it over. Later, we argued a little over what it meant to actually go to the symphony. For example, I wanted to go downtown, and she thought it might be just as good to go somewhere closer to where we live.

Eventually, with life and work, with kids and responsibilities, and because we didn't immediately act on the initial prompting, we forgot about it for a while. Occasionally, the topic would pop up in conversation, especially as I reviewed other things in my promptings journal. However, because it wasn't pressing, and it was frankly a bit odd, I regret to say that I, through neglect and delay, ended up effectively ignoring the prompting.

A short time later, because of the COVID-19 virus, the city and state in which I live issued guidance that people may not gather together in large groups. They directed that all but essential businesses be shut down in order to contain the virus.

Then, I could not, even if I wanted to, take my kids to the symphony or even out to eat.

This potential wonderful memory, this good time with my family, was missed due to my not quickly following the prompting.

I could never have guessed in December 2019 that there would be a virus that would shut down the world so quickly. In December, I could travel freely and do just about anything I want. Then, just a few months later, the world changed.

Another story:

On December 3, 2019 (the day after I felt prompted to take my kids to the symphony), I wrote the following in my promptings journal:

"Visit Grandpa, get all the stories I can from him. Bring Grandpa written notes of love and caring."

On this one, I "kind of" followed the prompting. I did visit him and took my children to visit him, but I did not "get all the stories I can from him," nor did I bring him "written notes of love and caring."

Grandpa has now passed away, and I lost my opportunity to get all the stories I can from him.

When promptings aren't followed, opportunities are lost.

Now, on a more positive note, since I ended the last paragraph, my six-year-old daughter and my seven-year-old son asked me if I wanted to come to the "school" they had set up in my daughter's room. Recently, I had the prompting to spend more time with both my daughter and my son, and today I intend to follow that prompting.

As today is Saturday, I am now sitting in my daughter's room playing school as I write this. Right now, I am in "practice" time, and she told me that I could use "practice" time to type on my computer. My daughter gave me a tour of the school (her room), with an "art center," "reading center," "playing center," and other school stuff set up strategically around the room. My wife and I smiled as my daughter read to us the schedule that she would have us go through today. I smile as I raise my hand like a schoolboy and call her "Miss Anderson" and ask her what I need to do next in school.

And now my daughter has notified me that "practice time" is over, so I have to go . . .

Now I've just finished visiting the "art center," "reading center," "playing center," and doing scratch art with my daughter and two of my sons. We read, played Uno, learned "codes," and practiced spelling. My daughter was delighted that I was writing a story about "her" school. It has been so fun. I am grateful that I can spend time with my kids. I am also grateful for promptings that help me do the most important things.

Also, I have been prompted numerous times to write this book, and I am following that right now.

It is important that we follow the promptings we get. We will get more if we follow them. If we ignore them, they will likely diminish or even possibly cease.

Later, my daughter asked me and continues to ask me if I will include this portion in my book, and I let her know that indeed, I will. :-)

Focus Brings Freedom

One of the biggest tools of the devil is distraction. You have gifts that only you can share with the world. You have a light. God wants you to share that light. The devil wants to distract you from it.

In the book *The Screwtape Letters*, a master devil is trying to train his apprentice nephew on how to tempt people.

In the excerpt below, he shows his devil nephew how distraction can be such a huge tool for devils, especially when people are trying to avoid doing what they know they should do:

> As this condition becomes more fully established, you will be gradually freed from the tiresome business of providing Pleasures as temptations . . . you will find that anything or nothing is sufficient to attract his wandering attention. You no longer need a good book, which he really likes, to keep him from his prayers or his work or his sleep; a column of advertisements in yesterday's paper will do. You can make him waste his time . . . and *nothing* given in return, so that at least he may say, as one of my own patients said on his arrival down here, 'I now see that I spent most of my life in doing *neither* what I ought *nor* what I liked.' The Christians describe the Enemy [God] as one 'without whom Nothing is strong.'

> And Nothing is very strong: strong enough to steal away
> a man's best years not in sweet sins but in a dreary
> flickering of the mind over it knows not what and knows
> not why, in the gratification of curiosities so feeble that
> the man is only half aware of them . . .
>
> It does not matter how small the sins are provided that
> their cumulative effect is to edge the man away from the
> Light and out into the Nothing.[129]

Again, one of the biggest tools of the devil is distraction, and as I write this, technology is one of the biggest distractions we currently have. I believe that this technology distraction will continue to increase in ways we haven't seen before, probably exponentially. It may be possible in the future to completely disconnect from reality in a sea of distractions and virtual reality.

Personally, I am unfortunately very familiar with technology distraction. I have wasted so much time reading the news when I could have been spending time with my children, working on this book, or providing for my family.

The problem with technology overuse is that it is self-reinforcing. Let me give you a personal example of a trap I fell into: I read the news to avoid doing the hard work of actually writing my book. I felt guilty for not writing my book, and so I read the news to avoid the pain of the guilt, which in turn caused more guilt, which in turn made it easier to read even more news to avoid the ever-increasing guilt. It was a downward spiral.

Here is the cure: Pray hard like it is all up to God, then work like it is all up to you, to stop wasting time. Ask for His strength to live here and now—in the sacred now. It is, at first, very painful to admit to yourself that you have given away years of your life to something simple, like the news, social media, or surfing on your phone. It is even more painful to continue to give your God-given life away to distractions.

Think of this. If you spend thirty minutes a day doing something, it really is much more than that. In fact, if you spend thirty minutes a day

---

129 Lewis, *The Screwtape Letters*, 59-60.

doing something, over the course of a lifetime you will have spent nearly two and a half years straight doing that thing (not including eight hours a night sleeping). That is all day, every day, no breaks, no weekends, sixteen hours a day, for almost two and a half years!

Do you really want to get to the end of your life and get the opportunity to tell God that, despite the talents and opportunities He gave you, you decided to read the news or social media for two and a half years or more! And that is only calculating using a half hour per day. I understand that most people are glued to their screens much, much more.

Are we willing to give up years of our God-given life for a TV show? Our phone screens? Playing phone games, watching news, playing Solitaire, or getting lost in virtual reality?

This book should have been written years ago. I have had so many promptings to write this book, and I have ignored many of them.

It is painful to admit it, but at some point, we get to account before God how we spent the time He gave us.

Remember that you really own nothing, not even your time. Time has been given to you from God. You are simply a steward. Use your time wisely and to help others. It will be painful and take energy at times, but keep at it and repent quickly.

Replace distraction with focus. Focus in on what you need to do and do it. Focused work moves mountains. Pray to God if you need help.

Work hard.

Focus.

It will be worth it.

Courage

Discouragement is one of the chief tools of the devil. The prefix *dis-* means to undo. The word *courage* means to be brave. Thus *discouragement* literally means to undo bravery. The devil does not like brave men and women. He wants us cowering in fear. The devil wants us to lose courage. When we sin, we lose courage. Sinning is like drinking discouragement.

What is the key to being less discouraged?

The key to countering discouragement is found in the scriptures: "Let virtue garnish thy thoughts unceasingly." In other words, be pure in thought. "And let thy bowels be full of charity toward all men."[130]

So the key to overcoming discouragement is twofold:

1) Keep your thoughts clean and virtuous. If they aren't, repent—as many times as you need. And keep repenting until you get good at keeping your thoughts clean.

2) Charity is Christ's love. Choose to love others the best you can as Christ would—even if you aren't feeling love at all. If you aren't feeling love for others? That's okay. Still love them anyway. Remember, love is an action word—a verb. Love is not a feeling. That said, if you

---

[130] Doctrine and Covenants 121:45-46.

start acting loving toward people, even when you aren't feeling it, your feelings will follow.

Remember, you can lead your feelings with your actions.

The strong, peaceful strength of Christ then comes in. This is Real Confidence.

Thoughts are Choices

I awoke one morning recently with a strange sensation in my chest. I could feel my chest fluttering in a very irregular pattern.

When I told my wife what was happening, she put her hand on my chest near my heart and felt the irregular fluttering and beating in my chest.

She, too, became concerned.

"Are you having heart palpitations?" she asked, worried.

Heart palpitations, I thought. *I am forty-two years old and much too young to be having heart problems.* Concerned, I called my father and spoke to him at length. Because of the COVID-19 virus, I decided that I should set up a "telehealth" meeting—in other words, a virtual online meeting with a real doctor through my cell phone.

I shared with the doctor what was happening. The doctor said it sounded like heart palpitations and told me that I should get into the Emergency Room or see a doctor right away.

I then called my aunt, who is a nurse in a different state, to tell her what I was experiencing. She told me that I should get to the ER soon.

Grumpy and frightened, I decided that I'd better take their advice. I was so stressed that I said some unkind things to my wife, and she, normally in a good mood but also a bit on edge, returned by saying some unkind things to me. The thought of having heart problems right in the middle of the COVID-19 crisis was stressing both me and my wife out.

Later that night, I drove down the nearly empty streets from my home to the emergency room. I went in and they hooked up an EKG machine to my chest, and the doctor put his hand on my chest.

He could feel the irregular beatings in my chest but while looking at the heart monitor said, "They aren't matching up."

Perplexed, I asked him what he meant.

"What I am seeing on the heart monitor and what I am feeling in your chest are not the same thing."

In less than a minute or so, he determined that the beatings in my chest were just a muscle spasm. And though he did think it a bit odd that the muscle spasms had been occurring all day, he assured me that my heart was fine—healthy, in fact.

My mood immediately lifted. I was thrilled that I didn't have heart problems.

My grumpiness and fear and the feelings that came from them were based on a lie. I had really believed that I was having heart problems, and my fear of heart problems and the related grumpiness that came from it were real. The emotions, however, were based on a thought that was *not* true.

Believe it or not, feelings are caused by thoughts—NOT the other way around.

My thought that I had heart problems eventually led to the feeling of fear, which I let lead me to act irritated toward my wife. This feeling was caused by a thought that probably went something like this:

I can't believe I have heart problems so young. I don't want this. I can't afford this. I don't need this right now. My wife probably doesn't even care what a big deal this is.

I was genuinely irritated and afraid. The irritation was caused by a thought that was not based on reality. It was based on untruth. I did *not* have heart problems, but my thoughts and even my "experience" said I did.

As soon as I found out that I really didn't have heart problems, my mood lifted.

So grateful that I don't have heart problems! I thought. Immediately, my mood changed from one of fear and irritation to one of relief and thankfulness.

The fear and irritation were based on thoughts that weren't even true. At *no point* during the day did I *actually* have heart problems, even though I *thought* I did. So, again, the feelings of fear and irritation at the situation were based on a thought—a thought that was a lie.

My feelings were real. But what was causing my feelings was not.

Here is the problem:

In marriages, in relationships, in work situations, people often make decisions based on feelings. Feelings are often good and based on truth. But more often than people think, they are not. Just as what was happening in my chest and what was happening on the heart monitor didn't match up, often our thoughts and thus feelings toward others don't match with what is *really* happening, even though it seems like it.

What thoughts do you have that are just not true?

Again, the feelings feel real, and they are indeed real. But what is causing the feelings, the thoughts beneath the feelings, are often not true.

My heart was the same both before and after I had the problem. The way I chose to act changed based on whether my thoughts lined up with the truth or not.

Ask yourself:

- *Are my thoughts about others true?*
- *What thoughts am I having that may not be true?*
- *Are my thoughts about my marriage and spouse and life and work and everything else all true?*
- *Really, really all true?*
- *Can I be certain they are true?*
- *Are even a part of my thoughts not true?*
- *How do I feel because of these thoughts?*
- *Can I find any evidence for opposing thoughts?*

· *Is it possible my thoughts about others are part of the problem?*

This leads us to the next truth: You can't always choose your circumstances, but you can always choose your reaction to those circumstances.

Let me give you an extreme example:

A private plane's engine has just exploded and caught on fire. The plane is now falling out of the sky and begins a slow twirl and dive to the ground. In the seeming chaos, one of the flight attendants is able to help you get a parachute on and tells you to jump out of the emergency exit.

Possible thoughts:

This is it. I am going to die. This is just my luck. Why do all the bad things seem to happen to me? I'm sure I am going to die.

Resulting feeling: dread, fear, resentment.

Another possible thought:

I can't believe that I get free skydiving thrown in with this flight. I sure am lucky! I don't even have to pay extra for this! I've always wanted to skydive anyway, and here is my chance! If I live through this, I might even be able to write a book about it—wow! How lucky!

Resulting feeling: excitement, gratitude.

Same situation.

Different thoughts.

Different feelings.

The nice thing is this: You always get to choose your thoughts.

You are the director of the stage in your mind. Stop letting things just come onto your stage without your permission. Start directing.

Here is another example:

"If my wife really cared about me, she would/wouldn't _____."

A thought like this could cause you to feel resentment. The truth is that it may just be a lie. In fact, many marriages have problems because the people in the marriages refuse to change their thoughts toward their partner. Eventually, the marriage falls into gridlock as both partners' thoughts fall into lies.

The problem is that the thought may or may not be based in reality. Maybe your wife shows love in a different way than you expect.

A more accurate thought could then be, "My wife sees things differently from me. She may care about me differently than I think she should."

Your thoughts are choices and can, with effort, be chosen. These small choices of what to think, and how to think about what happens to you, are huge, because from our thoughts the rest of life flows. Our thoughts create actions. Actions create habits. Habits create character. Character creates our destiny. Don't like what is happening? Change your thoughts. Analyze them.

Make sure that what is happening and what you are thinking match up.

Good consequences will follow.

Be Chaste and Virtuous

Jesus said: "I say unto you, That whosoever looketh on a woman to lust after her hath committed adultery with her already in his heart."[131]

It is not popular to be chaste and virtuous, but it is one of the most important things you can do. There are crazy good consequences for following this principle. There are very dangerous consequences for you and others for not following this principle.

Jesus said that we need to be chaste in our thoughts, not just our actions.

When we do align, we gain confidence: "Let virtue garnish thy thoughts unceasingly, then shall thy confidence wax strong."[132]

Having virtuous thoughts and having strong confidence are linked.

If you are struggling, don't give up. Keep working at it, even if you have to keep repenting hundreds of times. It is worth the effort to be chaste and virtuous.

---

[131] Matthew 5:28.
[132] Doctrine and Covenants 121:45.

Honor Your Spouse

Never berate your spouse in front of the children. Work on putting your spouse first, even before the children.

Ironically, putting your spouse first will actually help your children and their children in ways you may not realize.

They will see how you do put your wife or husband first, and they will have an amazing example for their own families in the future.

Elaine S. Dalton said:

> By the way you love her mother, you will teach your daughter about tenderness, loyalty, respect, compassion and devotion. She will learn from your example what to expect from young men and what qualities to seek in a future spouse.[133]

This applies to both wives and husbands, sons and daughters.

---

[133] Dalton, "Love Her Mother."

Start with Yourself First.

Start with changing yourself *first.*

This is so, so, so key.

For too many years, I would read something and then think about how it applied to others. I admit I still do this more than I should, and it has caused nothing but pain and strain on my relationships. All the good you learn in life will do no good if you are only applying it to others. Be brave enough to let go, to realize that God will teach others in His own way. Be brave enough to see what *you* have to work on—and then patiently start working on you. Give yourself time to learn, to fall down, to pick yourself up. You won't be perfect in this life, but just keep going and working on you. When you do work on you (the person you have the most influence with), your ability to influence others goes up, and the chances that someone else will change also go up. When you focus on the faults of others and neglect working on you, your ability to influence others goes down.

There are three things that are important when teaching others:

1) Example.

2) Example.

3) Example.

So, if you want people to work on themselves, *give them a good example of you working on you.*

1) Work on you.
2) Work on you.
3) Work on you.

Then:

1) Trust God and that the Light of Christ will teach all what they should do.
2) Trust God and that the Light of Christ will teach all what they should do.
3) Trust God and that the Light of Christ will teach all what they should do.

In fact, nothing will get better in any relationship until at least one or both parties take a good hard look at themselves *only* and determine that they will do all they can to love the other even if the other person doesn't return it.

It does not work to say,

"I will improve when they do."

Or,

"I am only treating them poorly because they are treating me poorly, and they deserve it."

Instead, the question should be:

"How can I love this person more?"

"How can I love them like Christ loves me? I don't deserve it, but He still loves me."

"Where is my extra silver?" (Remember the priest and Jean Valjean.)

"How can I show them mercy?"

I realize that this is very hard. I really do. I am not good at this, nor do I claim to be.

Christ said it even more firmly:

> And why beholdest thou the mote that is in thy brother's eye, but considerest not the beam that is in thine own eye? Or how wilt thou say to thy brother, Let me pull out the mote out of thine eye; and, behold, a beam is in thine own eye? Thou hypocrite, first cast out the beam

224

out of thine own eye; and then shalt thou see clearly to
cast out the mote out of thy brother's eye.[134]

If we are even beholding (which means "seeing") the mote in our brother's eye, we are in a bad spot.

It is so much better to start considering the beams in our own eyes.

I have found myself in danger more than once. I have been guilty of reading a book and thinking, "_____could use this" or "I wish he/she would read this—they are sure guilty of this."

Quite often, when something bothers us in someone else, it is because we are seeing a flaw that we have in ourselves.

An ancient leader told his son:

> And now, my son, I desire that ye should let these things trouble you no more, and only let your sins trouble you, with that trouble which shall bring you down unto repentance.[135]

Start with the person you can influence more than any other—you.

---

[134] Matthew 7:3-5.
[135] Alma 42:29.

Trust God

My sister, Shalissa Lindsay, wrote a book entitled, *Answers Will Come.* In it, she made clear that it would not make sense to worship a God you completely understood. If you completely understood Him, you would be on His level. Trust that He understands things you do not, and learn to be okay with not understanding all of His ways.[136]

Isaiah teaches this principle:

> For my thoughts are not your thoughts, neither are your ways my ways, saith the Lord. For as the heavens are higher than the earth, so are my ways higher than your ways, and my thoughts than your thoughts. For as the rain cometh down, and the snow from heaven, and returneth not thither, but watereth the earth, and maketh it bring forth and bud, that it may give seed to the sower, and bread to the eater: So shall my word be that goeth forth out of my mouth: it shall not return unto me void, but it shall accomplish that which I please, and it shall prosper in the thing whereto I sent it.[137]

These verses in Proverbs are key:

---

[136] Lindsay, Shalissa, *Answers Will Come,* (Covenant Communications, 2017).
[137] Isaiah 55:8–11.

Trust in the Lord with all thine heart; and lean not unto thine own understanding. In all thy ways acknowledge him, and he shall direct thy paths.[138]

---

[138] Proverbs 3:5–6.

Heaven Can Go Back in Time

I believe that repentance works in BOTH directions of time—Heaven works backward. Be brave enough to repent when you've made a mistake:

> 'Son,' he said, 'ye cannot in your present state understand eternity . . . That is what mortals misunderstand. They say of some temporal suffering, "No future bliss can make up for it," not knowing that Heaven, once attained, will work backwards and turn even that agony into a glory. And of some sinful pleasure they say "Let me have but *this* and I'll take the consequences": little dreaming how damnation will spread back and back into their past and contaminate the pleasure of the sin. Both processes begin even before death.'[139]

Also, consider this quote from Kyle S. McKay:

> Cancer often begins with a single cell, so small it can be seen only with a microscope. But it is capable of growing and spreading rapidly . . .

---

[139] Lewis, *The Great Divorce*, (Geoffrey Bles, 1945), 60.

As devastating as cancer is to the body, sin is even more devastating to the soul. Sin usually starts small—sometimes imperceptibly small—but it is capable of growing rapidly. It cankers, then cripples, then kills the soul. It is the major cause—indeed, the only cause—of spiritual death in all creation. The treatment for sin is repentance.[140]

Keep repenting.

Daily.

Pick yourself up. Be patient. Sometimes you have to repent hundreds of times or more—for the exact same thing—before you finally overcome it. Slow, incremental growth is good—it doesn't have to be fixed all at once.

Ask God for strength when it seems too hard. Focus on moving just an inch forward at a time. Just one inch.

Don't give up.

Keep going.

It will work out if you keep trying and keep repenting.

Don't be afraid to confess your sins—even if you have to go back dozens or even hundreds of times for the same thing.

Keep going.

---

[140] McKay, Kyle S., "A Mighty Change of Heart." (2020)

Do Good in Secret

Matthew 6 reads:

> Take heed that ye do not your alms before men, to be seen of them: otherwise ye have no reward of your Father which is in heaven. Therefore, when thou doest thine alms, do not sound a trumpet before thee, as the hypocrites do in the synagogues and in the streets, that they may have glory of men. Verily I say unto you, They have their reward. But when thou doest alms, let not thy left hand know what thy right hand doeth: That thine alms may be in secret: and thy Father which seeth in secret himself shall reward thee openly.[141]

There is a joy that comes from doing things for others that absolutely no one else knows about. That joy leaves when it is done to be seen of men.

Jesus, speaking of the Pharisees, warned:

> *But all their works they do for to be seen of men.*[142]

---

[141] Matthew 6:1–4.
[142] Matthew 23:2–5.

Be careful to not do your works to be seen of men. Do you feel you have to talk about the person you served? The service project you did?

Don't.

Keep it a secret.

Here is a test you might use to see if your choices are based on Conscience or Ego:

Am I wanting to do this to be seen of men? To be recognized? (Ego)

OR

Will I do this thing simply because I really want to care about someone? Will I do the right thing even if no one knows? (Conscience)

Do good.

Lots of good.

But do almost all of it in secret.

If you do let anyone know, let your children know some of it, but just enough to set an example for them so that they can teach their own children how to do good in secret too.

Remember, "No matter the question, love is the answer."

You Are the CEO of Your

Children's Education

Let me repeat that: You are the CEO of your children's education.

Do not let the system take over what God has trusted you with. The government does not own your children. The system does not own your children.

God has entrusted their hearts and minds to you, and you now have both the opportunity and the burden of making sure that they are educated in the best way possible.

This thought is not original to me.

In fact, I first heard it when speaking to my brother, Leland, who graduated with a master's degree in education from Harvard.

It is such an important way to think about things, and the best outcomes with education occur when parents proactively act as CEOs of their children's education. In other words, they take control and responsibility for their children's education.

Unfortunately, many parents have let their children's education fall to someone else, usually the state, the outside system, or some other government entity. They send their kids to school not really knowing what is going on in the classroom, not really caring, and then wonder years later why their children fall into trouble, get bullied, become susceptible to negative peer pressure, lose their faith, and have other major problems.

We have got to be more conscientious about this.

As the CEO, the buck stops with you. How well and what your children learn is 100% completely *your* responsibility—*not* the state's, *not* the church's, *not* anyone else but *you.*

Now, as the CEO, you may decide to outsource part of your children's education to a public or private school. You may decide to outsource part of their education to a violin or piano teacher, an ACT tutor, a karate master, or any of a number of outside sources.

But what you cannot afford to do is be asleep at the wheel.

If you do decide to outsource some of it to a public or private school, it would be wise to meet the staff, to become involved, to understand what your children will be experiencing. Remember that, as CEO, you have the right to cut off contractors who either are not aligned with your mission, are not performing, or have "gone off the rails."

I suspect that it will get more and more difficult for parents to raise their children outside "the system." This will make it more important than ever to have many, many conversations about what they are learning, and you, as the CEO of their education, may have to undo much of what "the system" does by making sure to talk it through with your children and inoculate them against false beliefs.

I suspect that much of what is said in this book about parenting, Christianity, and raising a traditional family, including this part about parents being the CEOs of their children's education, will become very unpopular. There is already a popular feeling that the government "owns" our children's education and that parents are simply useful as secondary caretakers. This movement will likely become much more prevalent, and though the word "own" likely won't be used, the concept will be strongly implied.

How do you counteract this movement?

Well, if you don't want your children raised by the system, look for other options. Perhaps there are alternatives to public schools—private or charter schools or a homeschooling group that you could join.

Don't be afraid to be CEO. God gave you this responsibility, and you can do it. Also, you will discover little things that can help you as you educate.

Here are a couple of examples of items to consider that may be comforting to you as you explore what to do yourself and what to outsource:

1) Research shows that in early childhood, intelligence is linked to the number of "turns" in a conversation that a child engages in. In other words, if you and your child are conversing and he says, "I don't understand how to do slopes in algebra," and then you say, "What about slopes don't you understand?" That is one turn in the conversation. The conversation turned from him speaking to you speaking.

Research shows that intelligence is correlated with how many turns there are in the conversation over time, especially in early childhood.[143]

So, to be a good teacher, talk to your children and let the conversation go back and forth from you to them and them to you as much as possible. In an hour or two, you will likely have more intelligent turns in a conversation than they would get in a typical seven-hour school day.

2) Let children hear a lot of words they don't understand yet. Research shows that raising children in a rich language environment is linked to positive outcomes.[144] You don't need to talk down to them. Let them learn new words. One of the hidden treasures of daily scripture study is that your children will be exposed to a lot of words, and you will be able to rapidly discuss and expand their vocabulary, building new neural pathways that will benefit much more than just their vocabulary skills.

These are just a couple of examples. You can rest assured that as you do your best to be a good teacher and to prayerfully ponder and

---

[143] Risley, Todd R. and Hart, Betty, *Meaningful Differences*, (Paul H. Brookes Publishing Co., 1995).

[144] Risley, *Meaningful Differences*

decide what is best for your own children, you will be blessed with guidance.

Learn what you need to know. Learn principles. Learn teaching techniques that align with those principles. Don't be overwhelmed by trying to make it perfect.

Then, teach your children. You can do it.

Effort

My dad used to say, "Work as if everything depends on you, and pray as if everything depends on the Lord."

Work.

  Hard.

    Pray.

      Hard.

The Lord will bless you when you do both.

The Stage of Your Mind

You are the director of the stage of your mind. Some refer to this as "the story you are telling yourself." The most important thing in life is not actually what is going on around you. Much more important is what you are allowing on the stage of your mind.

You can decide what is allowed onstage and what is not. The best way to get garbage off the stage is to put positive things on the stage.

It doesn't work to say, "Don't think about a pink elephant." Automatically, most will, just at the suggestion, think about a pink elephant. You have got to replace the thought about a pink elephant with a completely new thought. For example, start thinking of a white, sandy beach in Hawaii.

The Savior specifically warned about two things that we need to not let onto the stage of our mind.

The first was to not allow lust into our mind:

> Ye have heard that it was said by them of old time, Thou shalt not commit adultery: But I say unto you, That whosoever looketh on a woman to lust after her hath committed adultery with her already in his heart.[145]

---

[145] Matthew 5:27-28.

If you are struggling with an inappropriate or negative thought, don't sit there and try to not think about it. Instead, fill the stage with something else: For example, try praying and thanking God for all the blessings He has given you. Name each blessing one by one and keep going. Pray hard for assistance to be positive and make good choices. Then try filling your mind with positive music, scriptures, good articles, hymns, and so forth.

The bad thoughts will be crowded out by the good thoughts.

The second thing Christ warned against is anger toward others:

> But I say unto you, That whosoever is angry with his brother . . . shall be in danger of the judgment: and whosoever shall say to his brother, Raca, shall be in danger of the council: but whosoever shall say, Thou fool, shall be in danger of hell fire.[146]

Many times when we are angry, we focus again and again on the negative characteristics of another. We may play something that they did again and again in our head. It is at this time we can think, "Wow, what a great opportunity to practice loving like Jesus did."

Both anger and lust are things that are a result of our thoughts and actions.

It's hard to manage your thoughts. But almost everything worthwhile is hard.

---

[146] Matthew 5:22.

Confessing and Admitting Our Own Sins

It is when we notice the dirt that God is most present in us: it is the very sign of His presence.[147]

Admitting and confessing our own sins is a part of repentance. It sounds awful, and at first it can be, but it is really freeing, and really nothing can be done until you admit to God and the one hurt by your sin that there is a problem. Sometimes, some sins require confessing to a church leader.

Admitting that we are sinners and confessing that to God and others allows us to start the repentance process, and not much can be done until we admit we have a problem.

I am a sinner. I try to do what I preach but fall short much of the time. I need a Savior.

One of the biggest lies of the adversary is that you can do wrong and "it won't hurt anyone."

It always hurts someone, even if you cannot see it. Even sins that are done in "private" hurt others. Unrepented private sins, like all sins, spread like cancer. You cannot tell a "white lie" or steal something or look at pornography in secret and not repent of it and think that it won't

---

[147] Lewis, *Letters*, 470.

affect anyone. Your guilt and hiding, like it or not, will result in more sins being committed. Your mood around others will quickly sour, and you will begin treating people much more poorly than you would have if you had just quickly repented. Even if others don't know of the sin, the sin can and will affect them.

Let's repent as fast as we can.

Honor Your Father and Mother

Honor your father and mother. When your children see you honor your parents, it will set a pattern for them as well.

Making Friends

If you want to make friends, be *genuinely* interested in other people and listen more than you speak. It is natural to want to talk about yourself, but it is better to let the other person talk about themselves more. Remember, the one that is talking the most is the one that is enjoying the conversation the most.

My daughter taught me to go into a friendship seeking to serve, not to be served. Pretend that everyone you meet has a sign on their head that says, "Make me feel important," and then humbly treat everyone as if they are the most important person in the world. Learn their names. Use them. Then, be humble, and choose to be friends with all, not just people who are "in."

C.S. Lewis referred to the "in" crowd as "the inner ring" and said this about the desire to be "in":

> Unless you take measures to prevent it, this desire is going to be one of the chief motives of your life, from the first day on which you enter your profession until the day when you are too old to care . . .
>
> Of all passions the passion for the Inner Ring is most skillful in making a man who is not yet a very bad man do very bad things . . .

> Once the first novelty is worn off, the members of this
> circle will be no more interesting than your old friends.[148]

I had a dear friend who I was friends with for many years. When I was in my teenage years, I decided that I wanted to be more "popular" in high school and made many new friends. In part, I did this through learning most of the names of the people in my class and being friendly with them. I very badly wanted to be part of the "in" and popular crowd, and I found a way to do it.

However, I am ashamed to say that I stopped spending as much time with my old friend. Now that I am older, I realize the truth of C. S Lewis's statement. Being "in" really is a pleasure that cannot last. Sadly, as of the writing of this book, I have not been able to restore my relationship with this friend. Please don't make the same mistake that I made.

Beware of wanting to be in the "in" crowd. Believe it or not, this desire doesn't stop when you leave home or grow up. Many adults spend their entire lives trying to be "in."

Don't seek to be "in." Seek to love and really serve others—even, perhaps especially, those that seem lower in status in this world.

If you do this, you will have more friends than you thought possible, and you will be more like the Truest Friend there is.

---

[148] Lewis, *Weight of Glory*, 151, 154, 155

Be Still

Be still and know that I am God.[149]

Be still. Be quiet. Pray. Learn to meditate.

Try to do it daily. God can speak to you when you read scriptures, pray, and then are still and listen. Then, when you are still, often clear thoughts about what you need to do for yourself and to serve others can come to your mind.

If you have a prompting to do something—write it down.

Then do it.

I believe that these promptings can come best when we are still and quiet. It is easier to hear what God wants us to hear.

Having a daily time when we are quiet and then writing down the promptings that come to us can assist us in becoming instruments in the hands of Jesus.

---

[149] Psalm 46: 10

The Prerogative of the Brave

A coward is incapable of exhibiting love, it is the prerogative of the brave.[150]

To truly love someone means to do it without expecting them to love you back. Reciprocity, or karma—which is getting what you deserve—is not the love of the Real World. Love from the Real World is grace—love given even when it is not deserved. Loving others even when they don't deserve it takes strength and a whole bunch of bravery. It takes bravery because you may and likely will be rejected, repeatedly, maybe for a lifetime or more.

Do it anyway.

Remember, Real love doesn't fail.[151] Your efforts are not wasted. It may take much longer than you like, but it doesn't fail.

I almost titled this book *The Prerogative of the Brave*, because love is the answer—and to love takes bravery.

Be brave. Love everyone—even those who don't deserve it—and you will begin to become more like the Master, Jesus Christ.

The ability to love like Jesus is *everything* in the Real World.

If there is one thing I hope you get from reading this book, it is this:

Love is the answer, to everything.

---

[150] Gandhi, *Glorious Thoughts of Gandhi*, (New Book Society of India, 1965).
[151] 1 Corinthians 13:8.

And to get Real Love, we need to use our free will, and tons of bravery, to follow Jesus.

I love you, my dearest children. And I always, always will.

Christl

For whosoever shall be ashamed of me and of my words, of him shall the Son of man be ashamed, when he shall come in his own glory, and in his Father's, and of the holy angels.[152]

For I am not ashamed of the gospel of Christ: for it is the power of God unto salvation to every one that believeth.[153]

Christ is the way to the Real World.

Be a light that shines the way to Him.

I mentioned before that I believe that in your lifetime, there will likely be a maximum effort to confuse, discount, and counterfeit Jesus Christ.

Keep believing in Jesus anyway.

He is Real.

---

[152] Luke 9:26.
[153] Romans 1:16.

Books and Other Media

That I Recommend

The New Testament

Five Sermons in the Book of Matthew:

- Matthew 5–7 in particular (Sermon on the Mount)
- Matthew 10
- Matthew 13
- Matthew 18
- Matthew 23–25

Every book ever written by C.S. Lewis. That said, these are my favorites:

Mere Christianity

The Chronicles of Narnia

The Screwtape Letters

The Problem of Pain

"Plow in Hope" by Neal A. Maxwell

"Into the Burn" by Val Jo Anderson

For The Strength of Youth

The Power of Positive Parenting by Glenn Latham

Covey, Stephen R. *The Seven Habits of Highly Effective People* New York: Simon and Schuster, 1989.

The Eighth Habit by Stephen R. Covey

First Things First by Stephen R. Covey

Spiritual Roots of Human Relations by Stephen R. Covey (this is one I haven't read yet)

What's Behind the Research? by Brent Slife

Servant Marriage by Douglas Weiss

Works Cited

Attenborough, Richard, dir. *Gandhi*. 1982; Burbank, CA: RCA/Columbia Pictures Home Video.

"Benefits of Physical Activity." Center for Disease Control and Prevention. Accessed March 30, 2022. https://www.cdc.gov/physicalactivity/basics/pa-health/index.htm.

Covey, Stephen R. *The Seven Habits of Highly Effective People*. New York: Simon and Schuster, 1989.

Dalton, Elaine S. "Love Her Mother." *Ensign* or *Liahona*, November 2011.

Gandhi, Mahatma. *Glorious Thoughts of Gandhi: Being a Treasury of about Ten Thousand Valuable and Inspiring Thougths of Mahatma Gandhi, Classified Under Four Hundred Subjects*. New Book Society of India, 1965.

"Generation M2: Media in the Lives of 8- to 18-Year-Olds." Kaiser Family Foundation. January 2010. Accessed March 30, 2022. https://www.kff.org/wp-content/uploads/2013/01/8010.pdf.

Gibran, Kahlil. "On Children." *Poets.org*. Accessed March 30, 2022. https://poets.org/poem/children-1?mbd=1.

Gittleson, Kim. "Can a Company Live Forever?" BBC News. New York, January 19, 2012. Accessed March 16, 2022. https://www.bbc.com/news/business-16611040.

Hugo, Victor. *Les Miserables*. New York: Signet, 2013.

Holland, Josiah Gilbert. *A Dictionary of Quotations in Prose*. Edited by Anna L. Ward. New York: Thomas Y. Crowell & Co., 1889, 401.

Kerpen, Dave. "17 Quotes to Inspire Persistence." Inc.com. Accessed March 31, 2022. https://www.inc.com/dave-kerpen/17-quotes-to-inspire-persistence.html.

Kipling, Rudyard. "If–," *Rewards and Fairies*. New York: Charles Scribner's Sons, 1910, 200–201.

Lewis, C.S. *God in the Dock: Essays on Theology and Ethics.* New York: Harper One, 2014.

Lewis, C.S. *Letters of C.S. Lewis.* New York: HarperOne. 2017 (ebook).

Lewis, C.S. *Mere Christianity.* New York: Harper Collins, 2001.

Lewis, C.S. *Miracles.* New York: Collier Books, Macmillan Publishing Company, 1978.

Lewis, C.S. *The Case for Christianity.* Michigan: Macmillan Publishing Company, 1943.

Lewis, C.S. *The Four Loves.* New York: Harcourt, 1960.

Lewis, C.S. *The Great Divorce.* New York: Harper Collins, 2015.

Lewis, C.S. *The Last Battle.* New York: Collier Books, Macmillan Publishing Company, 1970.

Lewis, C.S. *The Problem of Pain.* New York: Harper Collins, 2001.

Lewis, C.S. *The Screwtape Letters.* New York: Harper Collins, 2015.

Lewis, C.S. *The Screwtape Letters*, Preface, p. x-xi. 1960.

Lewis, C.S. *The Weight of Glory.* New York: Harper Collins, 2001.

Liberto, Daniel. "Fear and Greed Index Definition." Investopedia. July 24, 2021. Accessed December 30, 2020, https://www.investopedia.com/terms/f/fear-and-greed-index.asp.

Lindsay, Shalissa. *Answers Will Come: Trusting the Lord in the Meantime.* Salt Lake City: Covenant Communications, 2017.

MacDonald, George, *Unspoken Sermons Series I,II, and III.* Start Publishing, LLC, 2012 (ebook).

Maxwell, Neal A. "Swallowed Up in the Will of the Father." *Ensign*, November 1995.

Maxwell, Neal A. "The Women of God." *Ensign*, May 1978.

Maxwell, Neal A. *Wherefore, Ye Must Press Forward.* Salt Lake City: Deseret Book, 1977. © Maxwell, Used by Permission of Deseret Book Company

McCulloch, J. E. *Home: The Savior of Civilization.* 1924. Quoted by David McKay in Conference Report, April 1935.

McKay, Kyle S. "A Mighty Change of Heart." *Ensign* or *Liahona*, April 2020.

Mother Teresa Quotes. "GoodReads." Accessed February 9, 2022. https://www.goodreads.com/quotes/550940-i-see-jesus-in-every-human-being-i-say-to

Nasiripour, Shahien. "Why Stanford MBAs Earn the Most." *Bloomberg Business Week. May 24, 2017. Accessed April 2, 2022.* https://www.bloomberg.com/news/articles/2017-05-23/why-stanford-mbas-earn-the-most

Oaks, Dallin H. "Parental Leadership in the Family." *Ensign*, June 1985.

Risley, Todd and Betty Hart. *Meaningful Differences in the Everyday Experience of Young American Children.* Paul H. Brookes Publishing Co., 1995.

Semega, Jessica L., and Kayla R. Fontenot, and Melissa A. Kollar. "Income and Poverty in the United States: 2016." *United States Census Bureau.* September 12, 2017. Accessed April 2, 2022. https://www.census.gov/library/publications/2017/demo/p60-259.html#:~:text=Median%20household%20income%20was%20%2459%2C039,increase%20in%20median%20household%20income

Slife, Brent, and Richard Williams. *What's Behind the Research? Discovering Hidden Assumptions in the Behavioral Sciences.* Thousand Oaks: SAGE Publications, 1995.

Smith, Joseph F. *Gospel Doctrine, 5th ed.* Salt Lake City: Deseret Book Co., 1939, 285. © Smith, Used by Permission of Deseret Book Company

Weiss, Douglas. *Servant Marriage.* Colorado Springs: Discovery Press, 2015.

About the Author

EksAyn is a believer in Jesus Christ.

He is also a husband, father, speaker and author.

EksAyn speaks nationally and has been seen on Forbes.com, Speaker Magazine, TV and various blogs and podcasts. His business book, *The Key to the Gate: Principles and Techniques to Get Past Gatekeepers to the Decision Maker*, has sold internationally. EksAyn has extensive business experience, including presenting to governments, associations, and other businesses. His educational background in psychology and life experiences have taught him how to connect and communicate in business.

More importantly, he is somewhat good at playing hide and go seek, jumping on a trampoline with his children, and at setting up a tent trailer when taking his family across the country. He also enjoys hiking mountains with his children, camping, reading, and learning about Jesus Christ.

EksAyn is on a mission to help as many fathers and mothers, marriages, and families as he can. He knows that what you do in your family can last longer and have far more influence than anything else you do.

Made in the USA
Las Vegas, NV
30 July 2022